The Tao of Shakespeare

A Book of Meditations

by Scott Kaiser

© 2014 by Scott Kaiser. All rights reserved.
No part of this publication may be reproduced
by any means, electronic, mechanical or otherwise,
without written permission of the author.

Muse of Fire Books
Ashland, Oregon

ScottKaiserShakespeare.com

Author photo: Jenny Graham

First printing: 2014
Printed in the United States of America

For my father, with forgiveness

PROLOGUE

My lifelong journey with Shakespeare began at age 15, when I played the role of Bottom in *A Midsummer Night's Dream* in high school. For an awkward teen, the thrill of embodying a Shakespearean character—especially a character beloved for making an ass of himself—was a life-altering experience.

From that time on, I became fascinated with Shakespeare and made it a personal goal to work on every play in the canon—all 38 of them. Had I been born in a Polish shtetl in the nineteenth-century, as were my ancestors, I imagine that my lifelong endeavor would have been a mastery of the Talmud, and the place of study, a yeshiva. But as an American, born in the twentieth century, that book was *The Complete Works of Shakespeare*, and the place of devotion, a theatre.

Most people don't think of the theatre as a spiritual practice, but, undeniably, it is. In fact, if you go all the way back to the roots of the ritual, to ancient Greece, the theater is one of the oldest spiritual practices known to man. For an act of theater, then and now, whether in Epidaurus or in Ashland, brings people together to share stories, seeking to learn about the purpose of life and how it should be lived.

Certainly Shakespeare, writing for his Wooden O on the South Bank of the Thames, understood this to be so. His later plays, the romances, in particular, were infused with spirituality. In *The Tempest*, for example, Prospero, reminded of his humanity by a spirit of the island, learns how to forgive his enemies. And in *The Winter's Tale*, Leontes, through faith, forgiveness, and 16 years of spiritual practice, is reunited with his dead wife.

But spirituality pervades Shakespeare's other genres as well. In the comedy *As You Like It*, for example, Duke Senior extols the virtues of a simple, pastoral life to his exiled followers among the trees of Arden. In the history of *King Richard the Second*, a deposed and isolated Richard seeks enlightenment through meditation in his dismal prison. And in *The Tragedy of King Lear*, Lear achieves spiritual enlightenment only after he has lost absolutely everything.

But I've gotten ahead of myself. Let me step back a bit…

For nearly three decades, working in classrooms, lecture halls, and rehearsal studios, in high schools, conservatories, and regional theatres, by writing, teaching, coaching, and directing, I've been making my living by helping people understand and interpret *The Complete Works*.

And nearly 40 years after I played Bottom, as voice and text director on a production of the rarely produced *King Henry the Eighth*, I achieved my goal of working on Shakespeare's entire canon.

You might think that's the end of the story, but it isn't. Because that's when the unexpected happened. No sooner had I reached my goal than my perspective on Shakespeare's body of work began to change.

For I began to notice something in Shakespeare's plays that I hadn't seen before. I began to discern, sprinkled generously throughout Shakespeare's writing, ideas that I recognized, from my days as a college undergraduate, as Taoism.

Now, before you get the wrong idea, I don't mean to suggest that Shakespeare was a Buddhist. Or that he meditated. Or that he was Lao-Tzu—the legendary author of the *Tao Te Ching*—reincarnated as an English glovemaker's son. Far too much nonsense about Shakespeare the man already exists in the world, and I have no wish to contribute to such fanciful thinking.

What I'm saying is this: The more I looked, the more I perceived a fascinating, elemental intersection between the wisdom of the ancient masters—Lao-Tzu, Chuang-Tzu, and the Buddha—and the wisdom of William Shakespeare.

For in both Shakespeare's *Complete Works* and in Lao Tzu's timeless *Tao Te Ching*, we see a veneration of nature, of living in harmony with the natural world.

We see a deep understanding of impermanence and the acceptance of change.

We see a reverence for love, with its power to heal, to embrace, to bind, to nourish, to sustain, and to enlighten.

We see an exaltation of human kindness: of forgiveness, of gratitude, of compassion, of generosity.

We see pleas for moderation and simplicity in all things—in living, in working, in speaking, in eating, in drinking.

We see a rejection of ambition—of the pursuit of wealth, goods, fame, accomplishment, power, reputation, and glory.

We see condemnation of violence, of aggression, of the abuse of position, of political corruption.

We see an admiration of patience, of meditation, of skill, of listening, of pausing before speaking, of acknowledging faults, of accepting flaws.

We see an affirmation of balance, of yielding, of cooperating, of coexisting, of seeking a middle way, of offering no resistance.

We see a rejection of absolutes, of judgment, of prejudice, of opinions, of negativity.

We see a censure of envy, of greed, of anger, of malice, of jealousy.

We see appeals for compassion, for humility, for mindfulness, for selflessness, for acceptance, and for honesty.

We see an acceptance of aging and death as a natural process.

We see a penchant for paradox, where truths are expressed in ways that seem absurd, nonsensical, enigmatic, self-contradictory.

In short, we see in these writings, despite the fact that they arose in different periods, from different places, in different languages, the exact same universal truths being expressed, truths that are "not of an age, but for all time."

Following this fresh path, I began collecting quotations from the canon, hundreds of them, gleaning them from my personal library of rehearsal notebooks—detailed records which contain notes from productions I've worked on at the Oregon Shakespeare Festival over 24 seasons.

I also immersed myself in Buddhist and Taoist literature by such authors as Herman Hesse, Eckhart Tolle, Stephen Mitchell, Pema Chödrön, Thich Nhat Hahn, and the Dalai Lama, digesting whatever I could get my hands on in my search for common ground.

With Shakespearean passages in hand, I would meditate on a quotation every day—mostly by walking along trails in the wooded hills of our small Southern Oregon town.

My intent, as I walked, was to find a quiet space where the stress of modern life, the words of William Shakespeare, and the wisdom of the ancient spiritual masters could all sit down in a circle and meditate together.

Returning home, I would transcribe my thoughts in the form of short poems written in free verse—inspired by Shakespeare's lines, reflecting upon modern life, shaped by the tenets of Taoism.

The collection of poems you now hold in your hands is the result of those meditations.

The process of writing this book has been enormously valuable to me in my quest to become a better, more enlightened human being.

I now offer these passages to you, gentle reader, in the hope that they may help you to find your own way on the path of life.

—*Scott Kaiser*

ACKNOWLEDGMENTS

I am deeply grateful for the contributions of the people in my life who made this book possible, namely: my wife Cathy, for walking alongside me on the path these many years; my daughter Rachel, for her irrepressible spirit; Amy Miller, for guiding the revisions, proofing the manuscript, creating the cover art, and skillfully navigating this vessel down the Amazon; Stephanie Kallos, for decades of enduring friendship; Sara Becker, for her unwavering support of my writing; Kit Bakke for her wise counsel on self-publishing; Beth Bardossi, for her artistic contributions; Jeffrey King, for his thoughtful feedback on the manuscript; Stephanie Evans, for her straightforward advice; and most of all, the authors and sages who inspired this book, in particular William Shakespeare and Lao Tzu—two minds that were not of an age, but for all time.

**"Modest doubt is called
The beacon of the wise."**

Hector, *Troilus and Cressida*, 2.2.15

When we are most certain
Of our opinions,

That is when
We are most likely
To lose our way;

For certitude,
Though it may seem
Like bright white light,

Is a kind of darkness
That causes us to stumble,
And sometimes fall,

Inadvertently hurting ourselves
Without ever seeing why;

Whereas,
When we are least certain
Of our opinions,

When we doubt
That we can ever
Truly know the truth,

The darkness of certitude
Is penetrated by the light
Of humility,

Making it possible for us
To navigate our way
Along the path to wisdom.

> **"For never any thing can be amiss,
> When simpleness and duty tender it."**
>
> Theseus, *A Midsummer Night's Dream*, 5.1.82

We each owe a duty
To ourselves,
To our children,
To our ancestors,
And to the earth.

Every day,
We can choose
To fulfill these duties
With simpleness:

For yourself,
Eat simple foods
And take a long walk;

For a child,
Offer an attentive ear
And unconditional love;

For your ancestors,
Light a candle
And share a memory;

For the earth,
Waste nothing
And leave no trace.

Simply follow this,
And nothing else
Can be amiss.

"I am gone, though I am here."

Beatrice, *Much Ado About Nothing*, 4.1.293

We all know
What it feels like

To be both here
And gone,

To be both present
And absent,

To be listening
But not hearing,

To be talking
But unaware of your words,

To be eating
But unaware of your food,

To be walking
But unaware of your surroundings,

Eyes open
But blind to the world;

Wide awake,
But dreaming,

Haunting our own lives
Like a ghost,

Yet, only one breath away
From coming back to life,

One inhalation away
From returning to the Now.

> **"We are blessed in the change."**
>
> Archbishop of Ely, *Henry V*, 1.1.37

We can expend
A great deal of energy
Dreading change—
Trying to keep things
Just the way they are
So that our lives will be simpler.

Imagine, though,
A life without change:

Imagine no sunrises
Or sunsets;

Imagine no billowing clouds,
Or gentle rainstorms,
Or harvest moons;

Imagine no spring bouquets,
Or summer rainbows,
Or autumn foliage,
Or winter snowdrifts;

Imagine no first steps,
No thirteenth birthdays,
No high school graduations,
No white silk weddings,
No giggling grandchildren—

How perfectly dreadful life would be!

By this, we can see how constant change—
Which we often fear and resist and curse—

Is actually one of life's
Great blessings.

"What's done cannot be undone."

                Lady Macbeth, *Macbeth*, 5.1.68

Like time,
Deeds move in only
One direction:

Just as an egg, once cracked,
Cannot be uncracked,

And a flower, once plucked,
Cannot be unplucked,

And a candle, once burned,
Cannot be unburned,

So, too,
A harsh word, once spoken,
Cannot be unsaid,

An unkind gesture, once displayed,
Cannot be unshown,

And a malicious act, once committed,
Cannot be unperformed.

And as this is so,
Isn't it better to be ever-mindful
Of what we say and do,

To practice non-saying
And non-doing,

Than to try in vain
To uncrack, unpluck, and unburn,

After all is said and done?

"There's a time for all things."

> Antipholus of Syracuse *The Comedy of Errors*, 2.2.65

Can you fly a kite
Without a breeze?

Can you find sea-stars
At high tide?

Can you spot constellations
In the middle of the day?

Can you build a snowman
In the heat of summer?

Can you pick flowers
In the chill of winter?

Of course not!
In all these instances
We understand that
Timing is everything.

Why then, in our lives
Do we fail to accept
That there's a time
For all things?

Why do we force things?
Muscle things?
Push against the flow?
Resist the will of nature?

Rather than simply wait
For the right time?

> "O Lord that lends me life,
> Lend me a heart replete with thankfulness!"
>
> King Henry, *Henry VI, Part Two*, 1.1.19

Being awake means
Expressing gratitude
At every moment,

Saying:
Thank you for this sunshine,
Thank you for this breeze,
Thank you for this tangerine
Thank you for this pair of shoes,
Thank you for that wagging tail,
Thank you for this stranger's smile,
Thank you for those deep blue eyes,
Thank you for this whiff of jasmine,
Thank you for that toddler's laugh,
Thank you for this pecan pie,
Thank you for this rising moon,
Thank you for these fireflies,
Thank you for this cozy bed—
Thank you for this thankfulness;

For perpetual gratitude
Is how we fill our hearts
With joy.

> "I as free forgive you
> As I would be forgiven. I forgive all."
>
> Buckingham, *Henry VIII*, 2.1.82

If we look deeply into Love's mirror
And dwell on the reflection,

We can clearly see that

When we stop hurting others
We stop hurting ourselves,

When we stop blaming others
We stop blaming ourselves,

When we reconcile with others
We reconcile with ourselves,

When are kind to others
We are kind to ourselves,

When we are generous with others
We are generous with ourselves,

When we feel compassion for others
We feel compassion for ourselves,

When we forgive others,
We forgive ourselves.

Such is the infinite power
Of Love's mirror

That she heals all things
Within her gaze.

"Things won are done, joy's soul lies in the doing."

Cressida, *Troilus and Cressida*, 1.2.287

The joy of accomplishment
Is often fleeting;

The real joy of any undertaking
Is in the undertaking itself—

In the planning of a thing,
In assembling materials,
In gathering our tools,
In the sweat of labor,
And in the pleasant pastime
Of practicing our skill;

These things enrich the soul,
Fill both waking hours and sleeping
With the delights of doing.

Once a project is done,
These joys quickly evaporate—

Like a morning dew
Kissed by the rising sun.

"Honest plain words best pierce the ear of grief."

Berowne, *Love's Labor's Lost*, 5.2.753

Expressing condolences can be difficult;

We think to ourselves:
What words
Can I possibly say
To convey my sorrow?

What thoughts
Can I possibly offer
That will ease the pain?

What eloquence
Can I possibly bestow
That would make things better?

In times of grief, however,
Grand eulogy is not required,

Nor soaring tributes,
Nor majestic poetry,
Nor heartfelt songs,

Just simple words will do—

The simpler the better,
And honest,
And true;

Or even better—
Stay close,
Listen well,
And say nothing at all.

**"Truth is truth
To the end of reckoning."**

Isabella, *Measure for Measure*, 5.1.45

We tend to think of the truth
As something we can know—
A fact that can be grasped
And turned over in the mind;

But the truth is,
Truth cannot be fathomed
By the human mind,

For there is only one truth:
The universal truth
Of the intelligence
Of the universe;

And as we are immersed
In this truth,
Made of this truth,
One with this truth,

Any truth
That can be reckoned
In our minds

Cannot be truth.

> **"Let time shape, and there an end."**
>
> Falstaff, *Henry IV, Part Two*, 3.2.332

No matter how much you say,
Or how much you fret,
Or how much you complain,

About the way things have gone,
Or the way things are going,
Or the ways things might go,

Nothing you can say
Can change the shape
Of things to come—

Only time can do that;

Might as well relax, then,
And let time do
What time does best.

"A friend should bear his friend's infirmities."

Cassius, *Julius Caesar*, 4.3.86

What is a true friend?
By what marks shall you know one?

A friend will commend your goodness,
While abiding your pettiness;

A friend will recognize your wisdom,
While suffering your foolishness;

A friend will respect your integrity,
While enduring your defects;

A friend will admire your virtues,
While forgiving your faults;

A friend will value your abilities,
While accepting your limitations;

A friend will appreciate your decency,
While tolerating your imperfections:

These are the marks of a true friend.

Are you a true friend to someone?
Are you a true friend to yourself?

> "The crow doth sing as sweetly as the lark
> When neither is attended."
>
> Portia, *The Merchant of Venice*, 5.1.102

Nature makes no distinction
Between beautiful and ugly:

The song of a crow
Is not more strident than
The song of a lark—
They both are what they are;

It is merely our opinions,
Our thoughts, our perceptions
That make the one seem harsh
And the other pleasant.

We must learn, therefore,
To listen with nature's ears
If we wish to hear each song
For what it truly is.

> **"O! I have suffered
> With those that I saw suffer."**
>
> Miranda, *The Tempest*, 1.2.5

Although we are experts
At closing off our hearts,

Making sure that nothing
Penetrates our emotional armor
So we can get
Through the day
Unscathed,

There are times when,
Unexpectedly,
Something gets through
To our soft core,

And we are touched
With compassion
For someone
We don't even know.

We see someone
Living on the street,
Or watch a tragedy
Unfold on the news,

And, out of the blue,
We feel what someone else feels,

Wishing we could do something
To relieve their suffering;

And suddenly,
In an instant,

We are awake.

> "The earth that's nature's mother is her tomb;
> What is her burying grave, that is her womb."
>
> Friar Lawrence, *Romeo and Juliet*, 2.3.9

Nature wastes nothing—

Everything she creates,
Everything she nurtures,
Everything she ripens,
Everything she provides,

Returns to her in time;

Only man—

Who desires more than he can use,
Who takes more than he can manage,
Who consumes more than he needs,
Who makes things that don't spoil—

Breaks the cycle
Of endless renewal

And disdains the way
Of nature.

"And am I thus rewarded?"

> Queen Katherine, *Henry VIII*, 3.1.133

We are taught
From a very young age
That good behavior
Will earn us a reward:

A gold star in class,
A sticker at the dentist,
An ice cream cone,
A trip to Funland;

As adults,
We endeavor under the same illusion:
That if we do the right things
We'll be entitled to a reward;

We think:
"If I just wait a little longer,
Try a little harder, do a little more,
I'll get my reward:
Then, life will be good;
Then, I'll be happy"—

And in doing so,
We rob ourselves
Of the joy of Now;

But if we could find
The gold star in Now;
Appreciate the sticker in Now;
Enjoy the ice cream cone of Now;
Delight in the Funland of Now;

Every moment of our lives
Could be our reward
For living well.

"A staff is quickly found to beat a dog."

Gloucester, *Henry VI, Part Two*, 3.1.171

When things go wrong,
We're often quick
To find someone to blame;

It can be challenging
To pause long enough
To ask yourself—

Is there really a need
To blame anyone at all?

> **"My heart is turned to stone; I strike it, and it hurts my hand."**
>
> Othello, *Othello*, 4.1.182

Life has a way
Of hardening our hearts:

To survive
The multiple cuts
Of a day's journey,

We petrify them,
Calcify them,
Numb them;

But, in turning our hearts to stone,
Do we not cause ourselves
More physical harm,
More spiritual suffering,

Than if we had dared expose
That tender organ
Naked and defenseless,
To all the world?

> "What fates impose, that men must needs abide;
> It boots not to resist both wind and tide."
>
> King Edward, *Henry VI, Part Three*, 4.3.58

A good sailor knows
That it is foolish

To sail directly into the wind,
To steer among shallows and rocks,
To raise anchor in a blinding fog,
To head out to sea in a storm.

As with the sailor,
We would be wise
To allow things to be—

To understand
That some obstacles
Are not meant to be resisted,

But must be accepted
As the way things are.

"I did but crave."

> Pericles, *Pericles*, 2.1.87

Every day,
We're bombarded by messages
Telling us what we need,
Urging us to buy,

Insisting that we have to have
The latest, the biggest,
The fastest, the best,

Showing us how these things
Will make us beautiful, desirable,
Thin, smart, cool, deliriously happy,

Driving us into a delusional cycle
Of wanting, obtaining, and forgetting,
So that enough is never enough.

But if we stop listening
To these relentless messages
Of acquisition and possession,

If we liberate ourselves
From the clamorous chains
Of continuous craving,

It becomes possible to see
That the more we crave,
The more we have,

The more we have,
The more we want,

And the more we want,
The more we suffer.

> "The web of our life is of a mingled yarn,
> good and ill together."
>
> First Lord, *All's Well That Ends Well*, 4.3.71

How would we know warmth
If not for cold?

How would we know day
If not for night?

How would we know sweetness
If not for bitterness?

How would we know our friends
If not for our enemies?

How would we know peace
If not for war?

How would we know kindness
If not for cruelty?

How would we know health
If not for sickness?

How would we know love
If not for hatred?

How would we know life
If not for death?

The good and the ill of life
Are inextricably woven together
Like a mingled yarn—

They cannot be untwined.

"Your wisdom is consumed in confidence."

Calphurnia, *Julius Caesar*, 2.2.49

How often our own confidence—
Certain that it knows—
Can lead us astray,

While our uncertainty—
Knowing that it doesn't know—
Can point us towards
The surest, safest course!

Our confidence—
Rather than advising caution—
Can spur us on to foolishness,

While our uncertainty—
Rather than leaping into action—
Can awaken our good judgment;

You may be confident, therefore,
That often it is better
To be filled with uncertainty
Than consumed with confidence.

> "Who doth ambition shun,
> And loves to live in the sun,
> Seeking the food he eats,
> And pleased with what he gets,
> Come hither, come hither, come hither!
> Here shall he see
> No enemy
> But winter and rough weather."
>
> Amiens, *As You Like It*, 2.5.38

Every day,
We receive an invitation of sorts—

This invitation
Doesn't come in the mail,
Or over the phone,
Or as a text message,
Or as an e-mail;

This invitation
Isn't sent via FedEx,
Isn't found on the web,
Or heard on the radio,
Or seen on TV;

This invitation is delivered
By the sun,
By the air,
By the trees,
By the clouds,
By the birds,
By every living thing around you:

The invitation
To live more simply.

"'Tis an ill cook that cannot lick his own fingers."

Servingman, *Romeo and Juliet*, 4.2.6

We're all very good
At cooking up "shoulds"
For other people to eat;

But whatever it is
You're cooking up for others,

Imagine if you were forced
To consume it yourself—

To chew it, swallow it, and digest it—

Would it be palatable?

"Men's faults do seldom to themselves appear."

"The Rape of Lucrece," 633

On the freeway of life,
Many of us behave
As if we owned the road,
Driving in a car
With a terrible blind spot—

Weaving, but
Shouting at the other guy
To stay in his damn lane!

Speeding, but
Muttering at a bus
Riding our tail;

Spewing fumes, but
Cursing the toxic exhaust
Of an eighteen-wheeler;

A brake-light out, but
Glaring at a scooter
Who didn't use his blinker;

Talking on the phone, but
Grumbling at a teen
With his music blaring;

And in this manner
We drive merrily along,
Blaming and judging,

While completely oblivious
To our own faults.

"Why, all delights are vain."

        Berowne, *Love's Labor's Lost*, 1.1.72

Look in your attic, in your basement, in your closets—
They're filled with things you had to have,
Things you thought would give you lasting pleasure;

Now, they collect dust.

We're led to believe,
Through a barrage of messages,
That all these things we frantically gather
Will give us endless pleasure,
Will make us thinner smarter healthier happier sexier,
Will bring us contentment,
Will end our suffering;

But the pursuit
Of these delights is vain—

For the more we pursue,
The greater is our pain.

> "I have
> **Immortal longings in me.**"
>
> Cleopatra, *Antony and Cleopatra*, 5.2.280

Rather than wishing
To live forever—

Which is, of course,
Impossible—

Imagine yourself
As a single link
In an endless, unbroken,
Eternal chain of creation:

In that thought
Lies immortality.

> "Now 'tis the spring, and weeds are shallow-rooted;
> Suffer them now, and they'll o'ergrow the garden."
>
> Queen Margaret, *Henry VI, Part Two*, 3.1.31

In the garden of our lives,
As in any garden,

There is a time for planting,
A time for pruning,
A time for fertilizing,
A time for watering,
And a time for harvesting.

There is also a time for weeding.

What are the weeds in your life?

Have you permitted them
To overrun the garden?

> **"Methinks I see these things with parted eye,
> When every thing seems double."**
>
> Hermia, *A Midsummer Night's Dream*, 4.1.189

Can you look at a pinecone
And see a towering evergreen?

Can you look at an old woman
And see a young girl?

Can you look at a deep lake
And see a mammoth glacier?

Can you look at a forest fire
And see a rebirth?

Can you look at a rushing river
And see a canyon?

Can you look at a faraway star
And see a bright sun?

Can you look at a rival
And see an ally?

Can you look at death
And see life?

It takes time and patience
To develop the ability

To see all things
With parted eye.

"It is the breathing time of day with me."

Hamlet, *Hamlet*, 5.2.174

Whether it be
A brisk walk,
A bicycle ride,
A bout with a punching bag,
A session on a treadmill,
A run in the country,
Laps in the pool,
Or sitting in meditation,

Getting in touch
With our breathing
Is a way of getting in touch
With ourselves,

A way of getting in touch
With the present,

A way of getting in touch
With compassion
For all living things.

Make time every day
To breathe in
And breathe out;

In...
Out...

Repeat as necessary.

"Past and to come seem best, things present worst."

Archbishop of York, *Henry IV, Part Two*, 1.3.108

Looking though old photographs,
It's so easy to marvel at
Our youth,
Our friends,
Our lovers,
Places we saw,
Things we did,
People we embraced;

Thinking ahead,
We naturally take delight
In imagining the future:
Trips to be taken,
Riches to be spent,
Comfort in retirement,
Happiness for our children.

Why is it that
The "Now" of our lives—
The ever-slipping present—
Is so hard to relish,
So difficult to savor,
So tough to appreciate?

"Forbear to judge, for we are sinners all."

King Henry, *Henry VI, Part Two*, 3.3.31

In that every one of us,
At one time or another,
Is—

Both generous and selfish,
Both wise and foolish,
Both polite and offensive,
Both compassionate and insensitive,
Both loving and hateful,
Both forgiving and vengeful,
Both careful and thoughtless,
Both nurturing and destructive,
Both modest and boastful,
Both kind and cruel,
Both saint and sinner—

The only prudent course
Is to refrain entirely
From judging others,

For the sooner we accept
That our natures
Are comprised of opposites,
And that we all must strive
To strike a balance,

The better off
Every one of us will be.

"Poor and content is rich, and rich enough."

Iago, *Othello*, 3.3.172

To a man without a place to sleep,
A hayloft is a king-sized bed;

To a man without a roof over his head,
A pup tent is a palace;

To a man without a penny to his name,
A ten-dollar bill is a fortune;

To a man without a next meal,
A bowl of soup is a feast;

Poverty and wealth
Are states of mind—

Little can be luxurious,
If it brings contentment.

> "Heat not a furnace for your foe so hot
> That it do singe yourself."
>
> Norfolk, *Henry VIII*, 1.1.140

Hatred for our enemies
Boils our blood,
Intoxicates our hearts,
Poisons our systems—
And to what end?

Is our enemy harmed
By our boiling blood?
Is he defeated
By our venomous hearts?
Is he overcome
With our poisonous looks?

Do we not rather
Harm ourselves?
Poison ourselves?
Burn ourselves
When we stoke the flames of hatred
With so much fuel?

> **"Striving to better, oft we mar what's well."**
>
> Albany, *King Lear*, 1.4.346

By adding
One more spoon of sugar
We made the lemonade too sweet;

By adding
One more splash of color
We made the room too loud;

By adding
One more descriptive word
We made the sentence too long;

By adding
One more invited guest
We made the table too small;

By adding
One more sordid detail
We made the joke too crass;

By adding
One more frilly layer
We made the dress too tawdry;

By adding
One more pair of shoes
We made the suitcase too heavy;

By adding
One more modest endeavor
We made our lives too complicated:

Know when to stop.

"What is this quintessence of dust?"

Hamlet, *Hamlet*, 2.2.308

If everything
In the universe—

Including human beings—

Is atomically composed
Of the same stardust
Released billions of years ago
In the big bang,

Then this assemblage of dust
That we call man
Is the immortal stuff
Of infinitely recycled stars,

Meaning,
We are the universe,
And the universe is us.

> **"The fashion wears out more apparel than the man."**
>
> Conrade, *Much Ado About Nothing*, 3.3.139

If we look in our closets,
We're likely to see
Lots of perfectly good clothing
Abandoned for being
Out of fashion—

For fashion follows
The prevailing opinion
About what should be worn
And how;

If we look in Nature's closet,
On the other hand,

We can see that,
Although she perpetually
Changes her clothing—

Trying on new things in the spring,
Adding color in the summer,
Shedding layers in the fall,
Wearing white in winter—

Nature's fashion
Is to waste nothing,
To reuse everything;

Which begs the question:

If we fashioned
What is fashionable
After nature's habits
Rather than man's,

What would our world look like?

> "The abuse of greatness is when it disjoins
> Remorse from power."
>
> Brutus, *Julius Caesar*, 2.1.18

We've seen it happen
Throughout history:

Whether it be
A cop on a beat,
A mayor of a town,
A CEO of a company,
A judge in a courtroom,
Or a president of a country,

Power goes to the head
And banishes compassion
From the heart.

When compassion
Evaporates in individuals
With power over
No one but themselves,
It's lamentable;

But when compassion
Is siphoned from the hearts
Of those who possess
The greatest power
To do the greatest good,

It's catastrophic.

"Pleasure and action make the hours seem short."

Iago, *Othello*, 2.3.379

The pliability of time
Can be felt

Whenever we
Lose ourselves
In simple tasks,

When we forget
Any notion of results,
And just do,

Plying a pleasurable skill,
Like chopping onions,
Knitting a scarf,
Polishing shoes,
Planting bulbs,
Stacking wood,

Until the walls between
The doer and the deed,
The skill and the skilled,
The act and the actor,
Fall away,

And time
Evaporates.

"O, reason not the need!"

    King Lear, *King Lear*, 2.4.264

Watch a stream flow downhill—
It needs no fittings, valves, or pumps
To do so;

Watch the trees sway in the breeze—
They need no oil, gas, or electricity
To do so;

Watch the moon rise on the horizon—
It needs no map, compass, or GPS
To do so;

Watch the clouds rolling overhead—
They need no plan, thought, or effort
To do so.

When, in our lives,
We flow like the stream,
Sway like the pine,
Rise like the moon,
Roll like the clouds,

There is nothing
That we need.

"So foul and fair a day I have not seen."

Macbeth, *Macbeth*, 1.3.38

A day both fair and foul?
How is this possible?

Perception makes it so.

To a farmer who needs water for his crops,
A rainy day is fair;
To a house painter who needs sunshine to work,
The same rainy day is foul.

To a child who longs to miss school,
A snowy day is fair;
To a commuter who needs to drive to work,
The same snowy day is foul.

To an office worker in an air-conditioned cubicle,
A hot, sunny day is fair;
To a highway worker laying down blacktop,
A hot, sunny day is foul.

The difference is not in the weather
But in the mind of the beholder.

"Ask your heart what it doth know."

    Isabella, *Measure for Measure*, 2.2.137

When we let the brain
Chatter on and on incessantly,
Sometimes the heart
Can't get a word in edgewise;

So, take a moment
To quiet the brain—

Ask it to take a break,
To get some fresh air,
To take a walk around the block,
Or to meander in the park;

Then ask the heart:
Do you have something you'd like to say?

I'm ready to listen.

> "What private griefs they have, alas, I know not,
> That made them do it."
>
> Mark Antony, *Julius Caesar*, 3.2.214

We can never really know
The hearts of others;

We can never really know
What suffering another person bears,
What misery they're burdened with,
What losses, what wrongs, or what adversity;

What we can know
Is that everyone suffers in some way,
Carries grief of some kind,
Has experienced loss,
Endured wrongs,
Weathered adversity;

Life cannot be lived
Without experiencing these things;

Compassion, therefore,
Should be the default mode
For dealing with others—

Especially when they do things
That we cannot immediately
Comprehend.

> "My mind is troubled, like a fountain stirred,
> And I myself see not the bottom of it."
>
> Achilles, *Troilus and Cressida*, 3.3.308

We think of our minds
As problem-solvers—

Ready to help us
Remember a name,
Or calculate a tip,
Or follow instructions;

But our minds
Are troublemakers, too—

Coming between us
And our own immediate experience

With an incessant stream of
Of judgments and opinions,

A repetitive soundtrack of
Assumptions and surmises,

A hazy curtain of
Comparisons and complaints,

Muddying the view
Of the here and now,

And making it impossible
To see with clarity,
And to enjoy

The pristine beauty
That is right in front of us.

"Kingdoms are clay."

Antony, *Antony and Cleopatra*, 1.1.35

After an earthquake,
Or a hurricane,
Or a tsunami,

The human mind struggles to accept
The scale and scope of the destruction,

For in the waste and devastation,
The core of our existence
Is shockingly exposed,
Stripped bare for all to see:

The fragility
Of our most solid structures,

The futility
Of our most ambitious endeavors,

The impermanence
Of our proudest accomplishments,

Brought even with the earth
From which all things emerge.

> **"Reputation is an idle and most false imposition, oft got without merit, and lost without deserving."**
>
> Iago, *Othello*, 2.3.268

It's very common
To want to be popular,
To wish to be admired,
To desire to be famous;

But to live our lives
Seeking these things
Is a deceptive snare:

For reputation
Is nothing more
Than the collective thoughts
Of other human beings,

Thoughts that often have
No relation whatsoever
To any actual merit,

And shift direction
In an instant,
Like the jet stream
And the ocean currents.

Common sense, then,
Should tell us
To let others
Think what they will,

While we spend our time
Seeking to gain merit,
Wanting to help others,
Wishing to leave no footprint,
Desiring to be wise.

"To teach a teacher ill beseemeth me."

Princess, *Love's Labor's Lost*, 2.1.108

In the classroom,
We learn early on

To respect the teacher,
Pay attention to our lessons,
Do our homework,

And apply ourselves every day
To improving our minds.

In life, then,
When difficult lessons come our way,
Why do we, all too often,

Damn the teacher,
Ditch our homework,
Deny the need for instruction,

And utterly fail
To apply ourselves
To improving our hearts?

> **"When clouds are seen, wise men put on their cloaks;**
> **When great leaves fall, then winter is at hand;**
> **When the sun sets, who doth not look for night?"**
>
> Third Citizen, *Richard III*, 2.3.32

Because change is inevitable—

Day will turn to night,
Sun will turn to rain,
Fall will turn to winter—

Those who accept change
As the way of the world,

Who embrace change
As the only true constant,

Who prepare for change
As the natural order of things,

Will never be caught off guard.

> **"Rumor is a pipe blown by surmises,
> jealousies, conjectures."**
>
> Rumor, *Henry IV, Part Two*, Induction, 15

Why do we gossip?

Why do we feel the need
To talk about people
Behind their backs?

Why do we feel compelled
To share our opinions
About other people's actions?

Why do we exchange guesses
About another person's
Feelings and intentions?

Why do we hunger
To hear of someone else's
Misery and misfortune?

Why do we take pleasure
In pretending to empathize
While we set out to denigrate?

Why do we trade stories
We know to be unkind,
Unreliable, or untrue?

If we look deep within ourselves
And answer these questions honestly,

We will lay down Rumor's flute
And stop playing his tunes,

Finding peace
In the silence that ensues.

> "This world's a city full of straying streets,
>   And death's the marketplace where each one meets."
>
>   Third Queen, *The Two Noble Kinsmen*, 1.5.15

Life is full of choices,
Full of paths and roads and streets,
Going in every direction—

So it's common
To feel lost along the way,
To feel as though
Your life has run off course.

At times like these,
When we feel disoriented,
Directionless, adrift,
It can be helpful
To relax with the idea

That it's actually impossible
To lose your way
In this bewildering city,

For all roads lead, inevitably,
To the same great intersection—

To the common marketplace
At the center of everything,

Where each of us will exchange
Our worn-out bodies

For eternity.

"There's no clock in the forest."

Orlando, *As You Like It*, 3.2.300

Among all the creatures on earth
We are the only sentient beings
That refuse to obey nature's rhythms:

We ignore sunrise and sunset,
Light our cities to mock the day,
Drink caffeine to keep ourselves alert,
Tweak time twice a year to delay the night,
Travel in the sky through multiple time zones,
Converse with people on the other side of the world,
Take sleeping pills to knock ourselves out,
Set alarms to wake ourselves up.

Disconnected from nature,
Our modern ways
Are regulated by the clock:
Supervised by seconds,
Administered by minutes,
Devoured by hours
Restrained by days.

Is it any wonder that we feel
That our lives
Are out of balance?

> "The fool doth think he is wise, but the wise man knows himself to be a fool."
>
> Touchstone, *As You Like It*, 5.1.31

Someone who speaks
With great confidence
And great authority
Can have a potent affect
On those who listen;

Yet, if history tells us anything,
It tells us that oftentimes
The person most certain
That his way is the right way,
That his view is the correct view,
That his truth is the only truth,
Is the biggest fool.

What history doesn't tell us—
Because humility prefers
Anonymity to fame—
Is that quite often
The person who is least certain,
Who considers
His experience inadequate,
His ignorance encyclopedic,
His judgment fallible,
And his view imperfect,

Is the wisest among us.

> **"Give every man thine ear, but few thy voice."**
>
> Polonius, *Hamlet*, 1.3.68

One of the greatest acts
Of generosity
That we can do for others
Is to simply listen—

Listen to our children,
Listen to our spouse,
Listen to our parents,
Listen to our friends,

But more than that—
Listen with patience,
Listen with compassion,
Listen with our entire body,
Listen with our whole attention,

But more than that—
Listen without judging,
Listen without interrupting,
Listen without commenting,
Listen without forming opinions,

But more than that—
Listen until we truly hear,
Listen until we truly see,
Listen until we truly feel,
Listen until we truly understand,

For listening,
Pure and simple,
Is a silent act of love.

"Was ever feather so lightly blown to and fro as this multitude?"

Jack Cade, *Henry VI, Part Two*, 4.8.55

Human beings are social creatures,
And as such, we tend to do
What the pack is doing—

We follow the herd:

We buy what others buy,
Dress as others dress,
Vote as others vote,
Drive what others drive,
Believe what others believe—
Blowing to and to fro
Like a feather in the wind.

To go one's own way
Can be a difficult proposition;

"He's an eccentric," they'll say,
"She's a strange one," they'll say;

But never mind what they say:

Ignore the herd,

Listen to your heart,

And follow your own path.

"Who is it that can tell me who I am?"

King Lear, *King Lear*, 1.4.230

True,
Your parents gave you a name
When you were born,
But—

What does the path call you when you walk on it?

What does the tree call you when you rest under it?

What does the river call you when you fish in it?

What do the clouds call you when you marvel at them?

What does the rain call you when it falls on you?

What does the apple call you when you consume it?

What does the sea call you when you swim in it?

What do the stars call you when you gaze at them?

What does the earth call you when you return to it?

Sometimes that which
Comes nearest to the truth
Has no name.

"Truth hath a quiet breast."

> Mowbray, *Richard II*, 1.3.96

Our minds
Lie to us constantly,

Telling us
We need this to be fulfilled,
Or that to be happy,
Or the other to be contented,

Keeping our chests
Pounding with adrenaline,
Straining to contain
Our perpetually restless hearts.

Only when we surrender
To life's few certainties—

That achievement is fleeting,
That happiness is uncapturable,
That power is passing,
That wealth is ephemeral,
That death is inevitable—

Can we walk through life
With a quiet breast,

With the inner-peace
That comes with

Embracing these
Simple truths.

> "**Are you sure**
> **That we are awake? It seems to me**
> **That yet we sleep, we dream.**"
>
>   Demetrius, *A Midsummer Night's Dream*, 4.1.192

Through much of our day,
We fail to be fully awake—

We lose ourselves
in our own illusory tunnel,

Listen to our thoughts
Ramble on in circles,

See things not present
As if they were solid,

Tell ourselves stories
Of unsettled scores,

Engage in arguments
With phantoms of fear,

Whisper our desires
To ghosts of hope.

How do we rouse ourselves
From such powerful daydreams?

Simply pay attention
To something here
And something now—

Like the clouds in the sky,
Or your daughter's voice,
Or the smell of pineapple,
Or the feel of cashmere,
Or the taste of cinnamon,

And awaken.

> **"Thou art not for the fashion of these times
> Where none will sweat but for promotion."**
>
> Orlando, *As You Like It*, 2.3.59

We live in a culture
Of relentless self-promotion—

A culture where a person's title
And material gains
Are taken as outward badges
Of value and success,

A culture where
Trumpeting your achievements
Is considered smart,

And taking credit
For your contributions
An absolute necessity
For getting ahead.

Is it any wonder, then,
That seeking contentment
Rather than advancement,

Opting for a spiritual life
Rather than a material life,

Preferring devotion
To promotion,

Would make one seem
Utterly unfashionable?

> **"The robbed that smiles steals something from the thief."**
>
> Duke, *Othello*, 1.3.208

If you can smile
When you've been robbed
As if a burden has been lifted,

If you can forget
The thing that has been taken
As if you never owned it at all,

If you can wish
The thief make good use of it
As if it meant nothing to you,

If you can find joy
In having one less thing
To worry about,

Then you can rob the thief
Of the satisfaction
Of making you his victim.

"The better part of valor is discretion."

Falstaff, *Henry IV, Part One*, 5.4.119

A man who knows
How to fight
When force is unavoidable,

How to engage the enemy
When combat is necessary,

How to defend himself
When violence is required,

Should be admired for his courage,
Esteemed for his skill,
Commended for his integrity;

But a man who knows
How to prevent a fight,
When weapons are at the ready,

How to keep the peace,
When the peace is fragile,

How to avert bloodshed,
When others are bloodthirsty,

How to humanize the enemy,
When others demonize him,

How to use discretion
When others are reckless,

Though he may win no medals,
Nor commendations, nor promotions,

Is a true man of valor.

> "Be absolute for death: either death or life
> Shall thereby be the sweeter."
>
> Duke, *Measure for Measure*, 3.1.5

If anything is absolute
In this life,
It's this:

Someday,
Every one of us,
Absolutely, positively,
Without question,
Is going to die.

How we choose to deal
With that absolute fact,
However,
Is up to us:

We can accept it,
And enjoy the sweetness of life
While we're living it,

Or we can resist it,
And make our life a misery

By trying to defy
Life's only absolute.

"Sweets grown common lose their dear delight."

    Sonnet 102, 12

How quickly
We take things for granted
If we see them every day!

A bowl of red raspberries,
Our daughter's beautiful face,
The touch of our lover's skin,
The sound of our mother's voice,
The smell of jasmine growing on a trellis—

What a blessing it is
To be present enough
To appreciate these things!

How quickly
Can these common, everyday things,
Suddenly, unexpectedly,
Become exceedingly rare,
Or forever lost!

How much we yearn then
To regain their precious sweetness!

"Wisely and slow; they stumble that run fast."

Friar Lawrence, *Romeo and Juliet*, 2.3.94

We tend to dread the empty spaces in our lives—
The tense silences, the awkward pauses,
The unscheduled moments—

So much so,
That we rush to fill up these empty spaces
With aimless thoughts, with mindless chatter,
With meaningless activity—

An emphatic approach to life that causes us
To think so much and push so hard and run so fast
That we stumble—

Wounding ourselves
And those around us
In the process;

Which, to prevent,

We must practice

The benefits of breathing,

The power of slowing down,

The wisdom of waiting,

The skill of listening,

The virtue of observing,

The usefulness of yielding,

Rather than always running running running
Till we fall.

**"O, that way madness lies; let me shun that!
No more of that."**

> King Lear, *King Lear*, 3.4.21

Though we know we shouldn't—
We absolutely shouldn't—
Still, we do;

We do the thing we know
Will make us mad:

We tell ourselves the same old story
We know will only anger us;

We rub raw the same old wound
In the same old way;

We choose to take
The same familiar path
That leads to suffering.

Fortunately,
Learning how to stop
Before venturing into a fog
In which we lose ourselves

Doesn't require
The discipline of a warrior,
Or the will power of a king;

It merely requires
That we see what we do,
Gently acknowledge it,
And resolve next time
To do something different.

> **"And ruined love, when it is built anew**
> **Grows fairer than at first, more strong, far greater."**
>
> Sonnet 119, 11

Just as a broken bone,
Set properly,
Heals itself stronger
Than it was at first,

So too, a relationship,
Having suffered
Arguments and disagreements,
Break-ups and separations,
Can, over time, heal stronger
Than it was at first—

If properly set
By a skillful physician;

And that physician
Is love.

"Smooth runs the water where the brook is deep."

Suffolk, *Henry VI, Part Two*, 3.1.53

Modern culture
Tends to worship the young,
To venerate the new,
To celebrate the next big thing,
To elevate
The bright, the quick, the sharp,
The muscular, the vigorous, the gorgeous.

However,
If you seek the profound,

Then you must worship the ancestral,
You must venerate the ageless,
Celebrate the time-honored,
Elevate experience, devotion, and mastery.

If you wish
To encounter the profound,
It is best to disregard
Where the water runs fast and rough,

And look instead
To where the brook runs
Smooth and deep.

> "What we have we prize not to the worth
> Whiles we enjoy it, but being lacked and lost,
> Why then we rack the value, then we find
> The virtue that possession would not show us
> While it was ours."
>
> Friar Francis, *Much Ado About Nothing*, 4.1.218

Because we tend
To take things for granted,

It's sometimes necessary
To lose something

Before we fully comprehend
What it meant to us—

Which presents an opportunity:

Rather than mourn the lack
Of something precious,

We can connect
With a profound sense
Of gratitude

For all the good things
And all the good people
That remain in our lives,

And be thankful
For the instruction
Provided by our loss.

"The strawberry grows underneath the nettle."

Bishop of Ely, *Henry V*, 1.1.60

Picking fruit requires care:

To acquire the sweet reward,
We often prick our fingers
On the thorns,
Or strain our backs
By reaching up for branches,
Or tweak our knees
While stooping to the ground.

So, too, in our lives:

To taste the sweetness of our being,
To enjoy it while it's ripe and juicy,
We have no choice
But to cope with the sharp thorns,
Tolerate the tall branches,
And kiss the hard ground
Of our human existence.

> **"What need the bridge much broader than the flood?"**
>
> Don Pedro, *Much Ado About Nothing*, 1.1.316

In our goal-oriented culture,
We often obsess over achievement—

Using more effort than is necessary,
Doing far more than is required,

In essence, building a bridge
Far longer than the river is wide;

But if we can stop each day
For just a few moments
To ask ourselves:

"Where in my life am I trying too hard?
Where am I doing too much?
Where are my efforts too great?
Where are my goals too ambitious?"

If we can calm our minds,
And listen carefully to our hearts,

The span of our lives can be lived
Just as easily
As stepping over

A small puddle.

> **"Opinion's but a fool that makes us scan**
> **The outward habit for the inward man."**
>
> Simonides, *Pericles*, 2.2.56

Qualities such as
An open mind,
A generous spirit,
And a compassionate heart

Cannot be seen
In the color of a tie,
The length of a hem,
The cut of a lapel,
The bias of a dress,
Or the shape of a heel—

These qualities
Can only be revealed
Through deeds over time.

What terrible fools
We make of ourselves
When we form our opinions
Of other human beings

By scanning
Their outward appearance,

Rather than waiting
For their inward qualities

To unveil themselves.

> "**Who shall be true to us,
> When we are so unsecret to ourselves?**"
>
> Cressida, *Troilus and Cressida*, 3.2.124

Sometimes we can be
Our own worst enemy—

We lie to ourselves,
Cheat ourselves,
Betray ourselves,
Hurt ourselves,
Insult ourselves,
Abuse ourselves,
Delude ourselves.

How difficult it is
To find our way along the path
When such a virulent enemy—

An enemy who knows
Our every weakness—

Thwarts us at every turn!

The only way to fight
This enemy within our ranks
Is with kindness for ourselves,
With patience for ourselves,
With compassion for ourselves,

Turning our worst enemy
Into our faithful friend
And trusted ally.

"Travelers must be content."

    Touchstone, *As You Like It*, 2.4.18

Traveling nowadays,
Whether by air, sea, or land,
Can seem arduous, distressing, intolerable—

And for this reason,
Many choose to avoid a voyage
Rather than submit to travel's indignities.

Yet, in a sense—
Whether we venture forth into the world,
Or spend our days sprawled out on the sofa—
We are all travelers, of a sort,

And on this brief, one-way excursion,
It's better to pack light.

So leave behind the heavy bags of arrogance;

Leave behind the overcoat of fear;

Leave behind the firearms of anger;

Leave behind the jewelry of pride;

Leave behind the sharp knives of jealousy;

Leave behind the credit cards of craving;

For the less we carry on the journey,
The less we'll suffer as we go,
And the better chance that we'll find joy

As we approach our final destination.

"What's mine is yours, and what is yours is mine."

Duke, *Measure for Measure*, 5.1.537

If we cut our left hand—
Injure it so badly
That blood flows from an open gash,

Our right hand rushes
To the assistance of the left
Without hesitation.

It doesn't stop to think
"What's in it for me?"
Or "That's not my problem!"

For the right hand knows
That what happens to the left
Also happens to the right,

That the blood flowing
From the left hand
Is the blood of the right,

That right and left hand,
Though separate entities,
Are bound together as one.

So too, whenever we see
The suffering of another human being,
Rather than think
"I'd rather not get involved,"

We can view the suffering of another
As if it were our own,

And like the right hand to the left,
Without hesitation,
Offer our assistance.

"I am not that I play."

       Viola, *Twelfth Night*, 1.5.184

We play many roles throughout our lives—
Such as mother, wife, daughter, friend.

After years of rehearsals
We assume these roles easily,

Play them with skill,
And perform them with grace;

But, in the end, these roles
Are not who we are.

Though we cast ourselves
In these roles
To define our relationships
With others,

It is our relationship
With the universe
That truly defines us—

Our connection to the continuum,
Our bond to the boundless,
Our ties to the eternal,

That truly expresses
Who we are.

Be sure to rehearse that role, too.

"I will not choose what many men desire."

Arragon, *The Merchant of Venice*, 2.9.31

Advertisers know that

We want what others own,
Value what others possess,
Crave what others control,

So they continually
Put desirable things
In front of us.

But chasing
What the masses want
Leads inevitably
To poverty—

Not only
Poverty of the purse
And poverty of the wallet,

But poverty of the spirit.

For this reason,
We need to make a choice:

To want not owning,
To value not possessing,
To crave not controlling,

For this is the way to obtain
What all men truly desire:

Contentment.

"To show our simple skill,
  That is the true beginning of our end."

> Peter Quince, *A Midsummer Night's Dream*, 5.1.110

We all have things we like to do—
Things we've become so good at,
That we can very easily
Lose ourselves in them.

Whether it's knitting a scarf,
Swimming laps in a pool,
Or cooking a stew,

We experience the sensation
Of losing track of time,
Of immersing ourselves so completely
That we become the skill,
And the skill becomes us.

In these instances—
Whether it be hemming a skirt,
Fixing a car, or running a marathon—

A certain mindlessness takes over,
Where there is no past to replay,
No future to foresee,
No goal to attain,

Only the sublime simplicity
Of the present execution of our skill.

This is meditation in action,
This is the detachment of mastery,

This is the serenity of skill.

"Do not think so, you shall not find it so."

Prince Henry, *Henry IV, Part One*, 3.2.129

We know not to believe everything
We read in the paper;

We know not to believe everything
We see on TV;

We know not to believe everything
We hear from our friends;

We know not to believe everything
We see on the web:

These are things we come to understand
As we get older.

But do we know not to believe
What our own minds tell us?

Do we know not to believe
Our own thoughts?

This takes even longer to understand.

Yet, when, at long last,
We realize how unreliable,
How erroneous,
How fictitious,
How misleading
Our own thoughts can be,

We finally know something
That can truly be believed.

"Uneasy lies the head that wears a crown."

King Henry, *Henry IV, Part Two*, 3.1.31

We strive for success,
Yet it keeps us awake;

We fight for power,
Yet it damages our hearts;

We push for achievement,
Yet it robs us of joy;

We campaign to lead,
Yet it stirs up our enemies;

We compete for wealth,
Yet it is never enough;

We angle for fame,
Yet it destroys our privacy;

We long to wear the crown,
Yet, in time, we discover
It is burdensome to wear—

Heavy, uncomfortable,
Exhausting, joyless;

So why not abdicate—

Resigning expectations,
Relinquishing ambitions,
Renouncing accomplishments—

And enjoy an ordinary life?

"I seek not to wax great by others' waning."

Iden, *Henry VI, Part Two*, 4.10.20

We sometimes look with envy
At those who have more than us—

More money and possessions,
More power and privilege,
More comfort and security—

And in our darkest moments,
We may even find ourselves
Wishing for some misfortune
To push them off
Their high-and-mighty perches.

But wishing ill
Upon the heads of others
So we can
Feel good about ourselves
Is utterly self-destructive,

For, in wishing harm
To others,
We harm no one
But ourselves.

"Nothing can we call our own but death."

King Richard, *Richard II*, 3.2.152

Though we have

Closets full of clothing,
Basements loaded with crates,
Garages crammed with gear,
Boxes strewn with jewelry,
Shelves glowing with trophies,
Homes bursting with furniture,
Folders loaded with receipts,

There's only one thing
That truly belongs to us,

Only one thing in life
That's truly ours.

It is given to us
At the moment of our birth

And we keep it with us
Every moment of our lives—

Until that inevitable moment
When all of our lifeless things

Outlive us.

> "Wind, rain, and thunder, remember earthly man
> Is but a substance that must yield to you;
> And I (as fits my nature) do obey you."
>
> Pericles, *Pericles*, 2.1.2

In our obsessive quest
To dominate nature—

To dam her rivers,
To farm her forests,
To mine her mountains,
To extract her treasures
From well below her surface—

We often forget
That nature
Is not subject to man,

But rather,
Man is subject
To nature—

That is,
Until earthquakes,
Tsunamis, hurricanes,
Tornados, and firestorms
Remind us

Just who is seated
In the royal throne,

And who attends
On bended knee.

"There are no tricks in plain and simple faith."

Brutus, *Julius Caesar*, 4.2.22

There's simply no way around it:

We can't pretend,
Or hope for the best,
Or wait for a better time,

We can't write a check,
Or send a friend in our place,
Or crib from someone else's notes,

We have to have faith—

Faith that taking the time
For spiritual practice
Will help us to grow,

Faith that, with patience,
We can learn how
To let go of the past,
To let go of our fears,
To let go of our anger,

Faith that,
With kindness,
With compassion,
And with mindfulness,

We can understand how
To live our lives
In the here and now,

As we walk along
The plain and simple path
Towards wisdom.

"What cannot be eschewed must be embraced."

Page, *The Merry Wives of Windsor*, 5.5.237

There are so many things about our lives
We cannot choose:

We cannot choose our parents,
Nor the way that we were raised,

We cannot choose our family—
Our brothers and sisters and aunts and uncles,

We cannot choose our bodies—
Our height and the color of our skin,

We cannot choose our talents—
The ability to sing or solve a tough equation,

We cannot pick the weather of the day
Or the cycling of seasons,

We cannot decide what other people
Think and do and say,

We cannot avoid our unrelenting march
From youth to age;

And as this is so,
The wisest choice that we can make

Is to embrace those things
Which cannot be emended,

To stop fighting and resisting
What cannot be avoided,

In order to make peace
With ourselves.

> "Unaccommodated man is no more but such a poor, bare, forked animal."
>
> King Lear, *King Lear*, 3.4.106

Even when we look at ourselves
Standing utterly naked
In the mirror,
We fail to see the obvious:

That we are no more than animals—

Creatures that are born
To breathe, eat, drink, pee,
Sleep, mate, age, and die
Like every other animal
On our planet—

For, as a species,
All the things we've invented,
All the things we accumulate
To make our lives soft and comfortable—

Our modern accommodations—

Cause us to suffer
Under the powerful delusion
That we are not a part of nature,
But separate from it,

A delusion
Which must be dissolved
Before one can live

An enlightened life.

"With mirth and laughter let old wrinkles come."

Gratiano, *The Merchant of Venice*, 1.1.80

Wouldn't it be wonderful

If smiling all day long
Wrinkled our faces?

If laughing constantly
Stooped our backs?

If being kind to others
Turned our hair gray?

If being carefree
Weakened our knees?

If generosity
Made our eyesight blur?

If forgiveness
Stiffened our joints?

If loving
Blunted our memories?

If joy
Dulled our hearing?

Then every outward sign of age
Would be an emblem

That our lives
Had been well-lived.

"There is no virtue like necessity."

John of Gaunt, *Richard II*, 1.3.278

No raincoat?
A garbage bag can keep you dry;

No leaf blower?
A rake will serve quite nicely;

No swimming pool?
A garden hose will cool you off;

No air conditioner?
A window fan will do the trick;

No car?
A bicycle beats walking;

No place to sleep?
A hayloft beats the ground.

What we think we need,
And what we actually need
Are often worlds apart,

And the virtue
Of the simplest things
Is often overlooked,

Until they become
Necessities.

> "He's truly valiant that can wisely suffer
> The worst that man can breathe."
>
> First Senator, *Timon of Athens*, 3.5.31

It's extremely tempting,
When someone is in our face,
Blaming us, disparaging us, insulting us,
To fight back
With equally venomous
Speech and actions.

In this moment of temptation,
When someone is right in our face,
It is paramount to pause
Just long enough to ask ourselves:

Why should I
Provide a clear target
For my enemy?

Why should I
Commit to an offensive
Wherein I become more vulnerable?

Why should I
Double the aggression
Already in the room?

Why should I
Increase the suffering
Already in the world?

In a moment like this,
Is not the stronger course,
The wiser course,
The more valiant course,

Simply to yield?

"Men of few words are the best men."

Boy, *Henry V*, 3.2.36

Because most of us
Make a habit of talking
For the wrong reasons—

Flapping our jaws
Out of nervousness,
Or to show others what we know,
Or to prove our own worth,
Or to control the situation,
Or to build ourselves up,
Or to put others down,
Or to dodge responsibility,
Or to blame someone else,
Or to escape having to listen,
Or to avoid having to connect,
Or to hide our true thoughts,
Or to protect our soft hearts,
Or to obscure our true intentions,
Or to conceal our past actions,
Or to force our agenda—

The challenge is
To pause before speaking

In order to say
Only what is necessary,

And no more.

"Our content is our best having."

Old Lady, *Henry VIII*, 2.3.23

In a culture
Obsessed
With possessions,

With collecting treasures
That are quickly neglected,
And soon forgotten,

With obtaining
The latest, the newest,
And the finest
Of everything,

There's one treasure
That can be acquired
Only by letting go
Of all the others,

One possession
That makes possessing
Anything else
Unnecessary,

One valuable
That makes you value things
Just the way they are,

One belonging
That makes the whole world
Belong to you:

Contentment.

"Courage mounteth with occasion."

        Austria, *King John*, 2.1.82

The Latin root
Of the word "courage"
Is "cor"—
Meaning heart.

Courage, then,
Means more than just
The trait of bravery—
The ability to remain
Undeterred by danger or pain,

It means
A willingness to show your heart
In vulnerable situations:

The more vulnerable
A situation makes you feel,
The more courage is required.

So, rather than numb your heart
When unexpected situations
Or unpredictable human beings
Make you feel vulnerable,

Allow your courage
To rise to the occasion,

And show your heart.

"Of all base passions, fear is most accursed."

Joan de Pucelle, *Henry VI, Part One*, 5.2.18

In the catalogue of human emotions
Fear is the most confounding,

For, unlike other passions,
Only fear is the body's reaction
To what the mind imagines
Might happen,
Rather than what is;

For fear is the mind
Insistently asking the question:
"What if?"—
What if I lose my job? My home?
My dignity? My loved ones?
My health? My life?

And the body, ever dutiful to the mind,
Answers these inquiries
With stress, with tension,
With discomfort, with anxiety,
And sometimes with disease,

All of which can be avoided
If we take the time
To gently get acquainted
With our fears,

So that, when they arise in our minds,
We can take a breath, and say:

"No thank you, mind;
I have no need of what-ifs today;"

Then focus your attention back
On matters here and now.

**"If you be afeard to hear the worst,
  Then let the worst unheard fall on your head."**

Bastard, *King John*, 4.2.135

If we're afraid to hear of it,
Paralyzed by the thought of it,
Petrified to speak of it,

Then, inevitably,
When the worst is upon us,
We will be woefully unprepared;

Whereas,
If we live our days
Knowing that death
Is always close at hand,

If we keep death beside us
As we amble down the path,

Conversing with him along the way
Of love, of joy, and of virtue,

We can embrace our fated fall
Without anger, without regret,

And, best of all,
Without fear.

> "I see that Time's the king of men;
>   He's both their parent, and he is their grave,
>   And gives them what he will, not what they crave."
>
>   Pericles, *Pericles*, 2.3.45

In all the billions of years
Our universe has existed,

And all the billions of years
It will exist in the future,

We, who are alive today,
Will only see
The most infinitesimally small
Slice of Time's reign,

Whose supreme indifference
To the desires of men
As we pass briefly
Through his dominions

Should teach us
Not to squander
A single precious moment

Craving

What he has no intention
Of granting.

> **"Our very eyes**
> **Are sometimes, like our judgments, blind."**
>
> Imogen, *Cymbeline*, 4.2.301

In our daily lives,
During our waking hours,
How often do we actually
See the things that surround us?

Taste the food we put in our bellies?
Hear the sounds that fill the air around us?
Feel the things that touch our skin?
Smell the aromas that enter our nostrils?

More often than not
What we encounter,
As we go through the motions of our day,
Is our judgment of a thing
Rather than the thing itself:

"I don't like pink."
"I prefer the hot sauce."
"When will that child stop crying?"

And these same judgments—
That compare one thing to another,
That value one thing more than another,
That desire one thing over than another—

Keep us from seeing what is,
Keep us from accepting what is,
Keep us from embracing what is,
And endlessly trouble our hearts,

Making us blind.

"He is well paid that is well satisfied."

Portia, *The Merchant of Venice*, 4.1.415

While it feels satisfying
To get a paycheck—

To see how our time and efforts
Have been converted
Into legal tender—

Such satisfaction
Is momentary,
Short-lived,
Fleeting.

For true satisfaction
Cannot come in an envelope,
Cannot be saved
For a rainy day,
Cannot be traded
Like stocks and bonds.

True satisfaction only comes
When you can truly say:

"I would have done it for nothing."

"By my foes, sir, I profit in the knowledge of myself."

Feste, *Twelfth Night*, 5.1.19

Most of us curse our enemies
For making our lives more difficult—

For obstructing our way,
For provoking us, for vexing us,
For making us feel
Bitter, resentful, envious.

However,
Rather than curse our enemies,
We might consider for a moment
That there is reason
To be grateful to them—

For without our foes,
How would we know ourselves?
How would we know what pushes our buttons?
What sets us off? What infuriates us?

And without our foes,
How would we learn
To embrace patience?
To foster generosity?
To practice compassion?

If we take a moment
To think of our foes as teachers
Rather than as adversaries,

We might thank them
For the benefit
Of helping us
To know ourselves.

> **"In life's uncertain voyage, I will some kindness do them."**
>
> Timon, *Timon of Athens*, 5.1.202

No matter who we are,
No matter where we are
In life's voyage,

We all travel
In the same direction
Towards the same destination—

That is one of life's
Few certainties.

What is uncertain
Is how we'll treat everybody else
Along the way.

We can choose to push and shove
And elbow and knee our fellow travelers
As we walk side by side
To the front of the line,

Making ourselves miserable
In the process,

Or we can decide
To be kind to others
As we journey
To our common destination,

Making the voyage
More pleasant for everyone,

But especially
For ourselves.

> **"Those friends thou hast, and their adoption tried,
> Grapple them unto thy soul with hoops of steel."**
>
> Polonius, *Hamlet*, 1.3.62

If you think of yourself
As a piece of oak
Fashioned from a tree
Into a stave,

It's easy to see that,
As a single stave of oak,
You can hold nothing
On your own;

But if you gather
Other lengths of oak
And stand together
In a tight circle
Bound by hoops of steel,

It becomes possible
To store the sustenance
Of grain, flour, and corn,

And to preserve
Such precious items
As wine and whisky.

This goodly barrel is community,
Our trusted friends are the staves,
And the shared contents of the barrel

Are the spirits of joy
In times of plenty,

And a store of love
In times of need.

> "Nought's had, all's spent,
> Where our desire is got without content."
>
> Lady Macbeth, *Macbeth*, 3.2.4

That new designer purse?
Already out of fashion.

The new computer?
Already obsolete.

The new car?
Already dented.

The trip to Hawaii?
Still paying it off.

Contentment
That can be bought
Is fleeting;

Happiness
That can be purchased
Is short-lived;

To find true contentment
We must shop within ourselves.

> **"A very little little let us do
> And all is done."**
>
> Constable, *Henry V*, 4.2.33

Athletes often talk about
Being "in the zone"—
When practice vanishes,
And actions become effortless;

Actors talk about
Rehearsal melting away,
And suddenly, in performance,
Rather than playing the role,
The role is playing them;

Musicians talk about
The notes flowing through them
As if they were merely
A conduit for the sound,
As if they themselves
Were the instrument.

These experiences are not
Mystical states
Achievable only by humans
With exceptional abilities;

These are natural states
Available to everyone,
Achievable simply
By setting aside the self
And doing without doing.

> **"Happy are they that hear their detractions, and can put them to mending."**
>
> Benedick, *Much Ado About Nothing*, 2.3.229

Nobody likes to be criticized.

It's not easy to hear
That we made a mistake,
That we were in error,
That we might have done better,
That our ideas need rethinking.

Without feedback, though—
Either from others,
Or from ourselves—
How can we ever hope to learn?

And in the larger scheme of things,
Isn't it more important to learn,
To grow, and to improve,
Than to be proved right?

An honest assessment, therefore,
Should be accepted as a gift,
Rather than received as a wound;

For only by hearing of our faults
Can we advance—

Sharpen our ideas,
Hone our skills,
Liberate our minds,
Open our hearts—

As we move towards
The best version of ourselves.

> "I can easier teach twenty what were good
> to be done, than to be one of the twenty
> to follow mine own teaching."
>
> Portia, *The Merchant of Venice*, 1.2.15

If we pay close attention
As we go through our day,
We may notice a disparity
Between our ideals
And immediate situations:

Between what we say we believe
And what we actually do,

Between what we profess,
And how we behave.

That realization,
That understanding,
That awareness,
That a gap can arise
Between our beliefs
And our actions
Is an opportunity:

Being there,
Pausing there,
Lingering there
In that precarious chasm,
Feeling awkward and insecure,

Is the best possible teacher.

"We are not thieves, but men that much do want."

Banditti, *Timon of Athens*, 4.3.414

In a country of excess
Such as ours,

The dire need
Of those with nothing
Is often hidden
From those with much—

And dire need can lead,
In desperate times,
To desperate acts.

When those with so much
Deny a loving share
To those with so little,

Who is the true thief?
Who the true victim?

> **"Merry and tragical? Tedious and brief?**
> **That is hot ice and wondrous strange snow.**
> **How shall we find the concord of this discord?"**
>
> Theseus, *A Midsummer Night's Dream*, 5.1.60

When we're children,
We're taught to think of things
As having one quality or the opposite quality—

Things are either happy or sad,
Fast or slow, hot or cold, new or old.

But what we learned as children about opposites
Is not reflected in nature.

For in nature,

Things may contain their opposite
Rather than exclude them—
As a man carries genes from his mother;

And opposites may yield to one another—
As the dark side of a mountain
Becomes the sunlit side over the course of a day;

And opposites may support one another
Rather than conflict—
As an inoculation of a virus can keep us healthy;

And opposites may balance one another—
As every birth counterpoises a death.

In this we find
That the discord we feel
When we think of two opposites co-existing

Is actually the concord
Of the universe.

"Presume not that I am the thing I was."

King Henry, *Henry IV, Part Two*, 5.5.56

"Why have you changed your hair?
I loved it long."

"Why do you want to live there?
It's so far away!"

"Why would you want to do that?
There's no money in it!"

Oftentimes,
One of the biggest obstacles
To changing ourselves for the better
Is not our enemies,
But our own friends, families, and loved ones.

We all change every single day:

Accept that in yourself,
As well as in the people you love.

Presume that nothing today
Is the same as it was
Just yesterday,

Nor will it be
The same tomorrow
As it is today.

This is true for all things
Great and small,

But it is especially true
Of those we love.

> "With meditating that she must die once,
> I have the patience to endure it now."
>
> Brutus, *Julius Caesar*, 4.3.191

When a loved one dies,
The pain we suffer
Can seem unbearable,
Impossible to endure.

If we recall, however,
That the suffering
Of our loved one
Has come to an end,

We must acknowledge
That the pain we feel,
The tears we shed,
And the suffering we bear,
Is more about ourselves
Than the departed.

For our beloved
No longer weeps,
No longer suffers,
No longer grieves,
As we do.

We should rejoice, therefore,
Our dear one's passing,
And be patient with ourselves,

While we learn
To accept,
And to endure,
Their absence.

> "Choose out some secret place, some reverent room,
> More than thou hast, and with it joy thy life.
> So as thou liv'st in peace, die free from strife."
>
> King Henry, *Richard II*, 5.6.25

We all need a place where we can disconnect
From the modern world,

Where we can unplug all our devices
And set them aside,

Where we can take off our armor
And be who we are,

Where we can sit and empty our minds
Of all thoughts,

Where we can listen to nothing but the sound
Of our own breathing,

Where we can let our restless minds
Be still,

Where we can wake up to the present and embrace
What is,

Where we can be grateful for the delight
That is life,

Where we can move towards the end of the path
In peace.

"Jesters do oft prove prophets."

Regan, *King Lear*, 5.3.71

Jesters—
Or comedians, as we now call them—
Are the people we pay
To remind us
Not to take the world
Too seriously.

With silly bits,
Childish jokes,
Goofy sketches,
And absurd faces
They show us

That the things we know to be true
Are merely our opinions,

That the things we most prize
Are the most ephemeral,

That the things we take for granted
Are in a constant state of flux,

Helping us to laugh
At the foolish ways
We misunderstand
The ever-changing nature
Of our peculiar universe.

> "O God, that men should put an enemy in their mouths to steal away their brains!"
>
> Cassio, *Othello*, 2.3.288

We drink alcohol for pleasure—
To relax after work,
To lighten up at dinner,
To enjoy ourselves with friends,
To celebrate an occasion,
To escape our cares and sorrows.

But we shouldn't forget—
When we drink alcohol
We quite literally
Are poisoning ourselves—

Ingesting a toxin
That can not only
Steal away our brains,
But can also cause
Injury or death.

Drinking, therefore,
Is a perfect example
Of the constant need
For balance in life:

Knowing that in all things
There is a tipping point
Where something pleasurable,
Taken to excess,

Becomes poisonous
To our existence.

> "Thus play I in one person many people,
> And none contented."
>
> King Richard, *Richard II*, 5.5.31

In the "sandwich" years,
We can find ourselves playing
A multitude of roles simultaneously:

We play the role of parent
To our children;
The role of caregiver
To our parents;
The role of partner
To our spouse;
The role of employee
To our boss.

We've also been cast
In a number of smaller roles—
Supporting roles such as
Housekeeper, cook, gardener,
Nurse, chauffeur, handyman,
Trash collector, loan officer,
Financial advisor, computer programmer,
Massage therapist, and resident psychologist.

Of course, playing all these roles
Is fine, just fine, for the moment—

But what we really want,
What we really hope for,
Is the day we'll get the opportunity
To tackle the starring role
We've dreamed of all our lives—

The role of a contented
Me.

"A dog's obeyed in office."

King Lear, King Lear, 4.6.158

A set of keys,
An official's badge,
An officer's gun—

These are signs of power,
But not necessarily signs of judgment;

A judge's robes,
A Presidential seal,
A royal crown—

These are symbols of authority,
But not necessarily of competence;

An expensive suit,
A corner office,
A private jet—

These are marks of success,
But not necessarily of wisdom.

We should not surrender
To signs of power,

Nor blindly obey
Symbols of authority,

Nor be overly impressed
With the marks of success,

For when we empower
These trappings in others,

We cannot empower ourselves.

"But shall you on your knowledge find this way?"

Duke, *Measure for Measure*, 4.1.36

It is not knowledge
That helps us to navigate
The road to enlightenment,

For knowledge is like
A poorly drafted map —
Out of scale,
Missing landmarks,
Incorrectly labeled.

It is humility, rather
That shows us the way
To a place of wisdom,

For humility reminds us
That there is no map
To help us find
The true center of all things,

Only the eternal compass points
Of generosity, compassion,
Patience, and love.

> **"Thus the whirligig of time brings in his revenges."**
>
> Feste, *Twelfth Night*, 5.1.376

Because we are part of nature,
And all things in nature
Are cyclical,

What we put into this life,
One way or another,
Finds its way back to us,

So that,
When we hate,
We will be detested,

When we boast,
We will be humbled,

When we are selfish,
We will be lonesome,

When we are critical,
We will be judged,

When we are cruel,
We will be vilified,

When we are thoughtless,
We will be forgotten.

Thus the whirligig of time
Brings in his revenges.

> "All things that are,
>   Are with more spirit chasèd than enjoyed."
>
> Gratiano, *The Merchant of Venice*, 2.6.12

We are taught from a very early age
To set goals and to pursue them
With great vigor.

Whether it's a quest for knowledge,
A chase for fame,
A search for sex,
The pursuit of wealth,
Or the hunt for power—

We put these things in front of ourselves,
And run after them with all our might.

But in doing so,
We often forget
To enjoy the things
We already have.

We are so focused on the future,
So caught up in achieving
Our next goal,
That we completely disregard
Our present blessings;

And in doing so,
We make it impossible
For our minds to be at peace—

For a mind at peace
Is a mind without desire,

A mind that needs no more
Than precisely what it has.

"Nimble thought can jump both sea and land."

Sonnet 44, 7

The human mind is a marvel of nature—
It can solve complex problems
And imagine things that don't exist;

It has enabled us
To survive and thrive over the ages
While other creatures
Have declined and gone extinct.

Yet, the human mind,
With all its swiftness and agility,
Can be as much a burden as a blessing—

For the modern mind
Abhors the present.

It would rather sail in seas of memory,
Or fly towards a horizon of surmises,
Than spend a single moment
In the here and now.

The nimble human mind, therefore,
Like a wild colt, or fledgling falcon,
Must be trained
To do the bidding of its master;

It must be taught—
Though it can jump both sea and land—
To focus on this very step
Along the path.

> **"I never did repent for doing good,
> Nor shall not now."**
>
> Portia, *The Merchant of Venice*, 3.4.10

As we look back on our lives,
We can all remember

Selfish deeds
We wish we hadn't done,

And unkind words
We wish we hadn't spoken—

Actions and speech
That for one reason or another
We sorely regret;

But looking back on
Selfless deeds done
And kind words spoken

We feel neither remorse
Nor shame,

But rather
A warm feeling
Of contentment;

Which should teach us
That doing good for others
And doing good for ourselves

Is exactly the same thing,

And worth doing again
Right now.

"What great ones do, the less will prattle of."

Captain, *Twelfth Night*, 1.2.33

We spend a great deal
Of time and energy
Obsessing over the personal lives
Of celebrities and politicians,

Entertaining ourselves
With the affairs and troubles
Of wealthy, famous people
Whom we've never even met;

So it's worth pondering:

Why do we lavishly
Concern ourselves with those
Of great fame and wealth
Who have no need
Of our attention,

While we stubbornly resist
Lending our time and energy
To all the poor, anonymous souls
Who have great need
Of our attention?

> **"Take each man's censure, but reserve thy judgment."**
>
> Polonius, *Hamlet*, 1.3.69

When we accept
That no one can possess
The absolute truth;

When we understand
That it is more important to learn
Than to be proved right;

When we believe
That receiving criticism from others
Helps us to gain perspective;

When we welcome
The opinions of others
As a way to test our own;

When we recognize
That beliefs are not solid
But an expression of our desires;

When we make up our minds
About nothing,

And reserve our judgment
About everything;

Our hearts will find peace.

"What a piece of work is a man."

Hamlet, *Hamlet*, 2.2.303

The universe created man,
But despite what we may think,
We are not the be-all and the end-all
Of her creations.

While it is true
That we're a highly complex
And highly successful
Piece of work,

We are also highly flawed—
Enormously destructive,
Tremendously violent,
Senselessly greedy,
Needlessly wasteful.

Like the trilobites
And the dinosaurs,
We will have our time
As the dominant creation
On this planet,

But then we will be gone,
Making room for the universe
To experiment with
Another piece of work
To take our place.

All of which should remind us
To be grateful for the brief time
That each of us
Walks the face of the earth.

But more than that,
To be humble.

"My legs can keep no pace with my desires."

Hermia, *A Midsummer Night's Dream*, 3.2.445

Like racing greyhounds,
We chase our desires,
But we can never catch them—

The mind's mechanical hares
Are always faster, fleeter, stronger,
Than our mind's legs;

They will always outpace us,
Always surpass us,
Always upset us.

How, then, do we rout
These nimble and persistent rabbits
Racing in our minds?

Make a stand:
When the lure appears,
Refuse to chase it at all.

> **"A greater power than we can contradict**
> **Hath thwarted our intents."**
>
> Friar Lawrence, *Romeo and Juliet*, 5.3.153

Sometimes nature itself
Seems determined to oppose
Our best endeavors.

But is nature really to blame
If we build a house
On the beach
And it is destroyed by a hurricane?

Is nature really to blame
If we build a house
In the flood plain of a river
And it is submerged in water?

Is nature to blame
If we build a house
On a fragile hillside
And the land slides away in the rain?

When we build a house
Of expectations
On unnatural foundations,

Perhaps it is not nature
That thwarts our intents,
But the misguided nature of our intents
That thwart themselves.

> "O, let him pass! He hates him
> That would upon the rack of this tough world
> Stretch him out longer."
>
> Kent, *King Lear*, 5.3.314

With our miraculous advances
In modern medicine,
We've created a conundrum:

We have the means
To keep our loved ones
Alive on machines—

But is it compassionate to do so?

With all our expertise
In stretching out life,

Is it possible that death
Is sometimes the best medicine?

"Love's not Time's fool."

Sonnet 116, 9

Although Time
Reigns over our lives
With an iron fist,

Making us,
Mere mortals,
His pitiful fools,

Love does not bow
To Time's strict edicts,

Nor pay any heed
To Time's ceaseless commands,

For Love, being eternal,
Is everywhen at once;

Love, being immortal,
Is everywho at once;

Love, being supreme
Is everywhy at once;

Which is how Love omnipotent,
Boundless and infinite,

Binds the multiverse
And all things in it,

Obliging the tyrant Time
To bend his chronic knees

To softly kiss Love's
Sovereign ring.

**"Now I feed myself
With most delicious poison."**

Cleopatra, *Antony and Cleopatra*, 1.5.26

In the same way
That we consume
Sugar, salt, and fat,
Even though we know
They're bad for our bodies,

We regularly feed on
Greed, anger, and delusion,
Even though we know
They're poison to our spirits—

Greed, like fat,
Weighs us down with more than we need,
Saps our energy with insatiable craving,
Softens our resolve with seductive distractions;

Anger, like salt,
Clogs our arteries with loathing,
Raises our blood pressure with contempt,
Makes our hearts pump harder with hatred and hostility;

Delusion, like sugar,
Fills our stomachs with empty calories,
Fools us into thinking we're getting sustenance,
Tricks us into believing all things should be sweet;

Which shows us that,
Just as we need to eat well
To maintain our physical health,

We must learn to think well
To maintain our spiritual health.

"In sleep a king, but waking no such matter."

Sonnet 87, 14

It is sometimes said
That our nightly dreams
Are the shadows cast in our minds
By our most potent desires
And our most primal fears.

Each morning,
With the rising of the sun,
We awaken from our slumbers
And shake off these dreams,
Knowing them to be phantoms.

But many of us live
In a waking dream,
Where our desires
Cause us to see things
Not as they are,
But as we wish them to be,

In a walking slumber,
Where our fears
Cause us to see things
Not as they are,
But as we dread they shall be.

When dreaming in our beds,
We can rouse ourselves
From sleep;

But when dreaming on our feet,
How do we awaken?

> "To shame the guise of the world, I will begin
> The fashion: less without and more within."
>
> Posthumus, *Cymbeline*, 5.1.32

Our modern way of life
Is built on a foundation
Of more:

More bathrooms and shoes,
More choices and channels,
More features and servings,
More carats and gigabytes,
More closets and horsepower.

In such times,
Choosing less
May seem unfashionable;

Choosing simplicity
May seem strange;

Choosing to let go
May seem foolish;

Yet, in such times,
Choosing less without
And more within
May be the only way to obtain
An unfashionable, strange, and foolish

Contentment.

"Everyone can master a grief but he that has it."

Benedick, *Much Ado About Nothing*, 3.2.26

Strong feelings of empathy
For someone in grief
Will often move us

To give advice,
To offer guidance,
To propose fixes,
To suggest solutions—

Well-intentioned actions
Sprung from a desire
To relieve suffering
In another human being.

But where counsel is not sought,
And opinions not wanted,
Attempting to intervene
Can do more harm than good.

True compassion, therefore,
Should move us
To simply be present
With someone in grief,

Rather than urge them
To master it.

> **"How sharper than a serpent's tooth it is**
> **To have a thankless child."**
>
> King Lear, *King Lear*, 1.4.288

Truly, it stings
When our children forget
All of the time and energy,
All of the loving care
We heap upon them,

Forget to show gratitude
For all the years of nurturing—
All the tears and joy
We lavish on their growth.

Sadly, though,
It isn't always the fault
Of the child
That she knows not
How to say "thank you."

Sometimes,
We only have ourselves
To point the finger at—

Who forgot to teach
The art of thankfulness

By expressing it every day.

"I spake but by a metaphor."

Paroles, *All's Well That Ends Well*, 5.2.11

Because our emotions
Cannot be held,
Cannot be measured,
Cannot be dissected,

When we talk about our inner lives,
We must speak of them in metaphors,

Where we imagine
Our lust as a fire,
Our anger as a poison,
Our fear as a watchdog,
Our jealousy as a monster.

But when we talk about spiritual matters,
Even metaphors will fail us—

For there are things that can be known,
But not explained with language;
That can be understood,
But not described in words;
That can be experienced
But not articulated;
Felt, but not named.

In fact, the more profound
The spiritual truth,
The more unnamable it becomes,

Till it can only be expressed
Through silence.

> "Let me embrace thee, sour adversities,
> For wise men say it is the wisest course."
>
> King Henry, *Henry VI, Part Three*, 3.1.24

When swimmers,
Caught in an undertow,
Try to swim back to shore
Against the powerful force
Of the sea's current,
They often exhaust themselves
And drown;

But if they remain calm
And go with the flow
Of the rip current
Rather than fighting against it,

If they wait patiently
For the moment
When the insistent pull
Subsides,

They can swim parallel to the shore,
Then back to the beach to safety;

By which we can fathom
That the real danger presented
By any adverse situation

Is not the force of the tide
In which we find ourselves,
But how we react to it;

And that,
By resolving to embrace adversity
Rather than oppose it,

We choose the wisest course.

> "There are many events in the womb of time
> which will be delivered."
>
> Iago, *Othello*, 1.3.369

Expectant parents,
Although they know
Absolutely nothing
About the child
They are poised
To bring into the world,

Will fall in love
With that child
From the very moment
It is born.

In the same way,
Although we know
Absolutely nothing
About the events
Poised to emerge
From the womb
Of mother Time,

We must be prepared
To embrace with open arms
Whatever she delivers.

> "Even here will I put off my hope, and keep it
> No longer for my flatterer."
>
> Alonso, *The Tempest*, 3.3.8

Hope is a notorious flatterer.

In a sweet, seductive voice,
She tells us that one day
We'll achieve our heart's desires,

Promising us that we'll be rich,
Assuring us that we'll be secure,
Swearing that we'll be satisfied,
That we'll be happy, that we'll be loved.

Though Hope pleases us
By whispering these nothings
Into our all-too-credulous ears,
She cunningly misleads us
With satisfactions yet to come,

For all the lovely things
She promises so earnestly
Are merely phantoms of the future
That continually make
Our hearts ache
In the here and now.

Which is why the wisest course of action
Is to break things off with alluring Hope,

Telling her
That the only day
That I will ever have
Is today,

And that today is perfect
Exactly as it is.

"Seek to know no more."

Witches, *Macbeth*, 4.1.103

It's very human
To try to see
Into the future—

We all want to know
What's ahead on the road
So we can be prepared;

So much so,
That we regularly go
Beyond predicting,
And try to control the future,
Try to force events to come,

Hurting ourselves,
And others,
In the process;

Which, to avoid,
We must seek to know no more
Than this very moment,

For by trying to determine
Our future,

We continually injure
Our present.

> "I am bound
> Upon a wheel of fire, that mine own tears
> Do scald like molten lead."
>
> King Lear, *King Lear*, 4.7.45

Our own minds
Create the wheel;

Our delusions
Bind us to it;

Our habitual thoughts
Light the wheel on fire;

Our egos
Start it rolling;

Our responses to life
Give it momentum;

Our inability to stop
Keeps us suffering.

How do we free ourselves
From this self-made, blazing,
Wheel of fire?

First, we must learn
To see what we are doing—

And refrain.

> "To be, or not to be, that is the question:
> Whether 'tis nobler in the mind to suffer
> The slings and arrows of outrageous fortune,
> Or to take arms against a sea of troubles,
> And by opposing, end them."
>
> Hamlet, *Hamlet*, 3.1.55

The day may come
When we are suffering
With a terminal condition,

When we are facing
A painful, inexorable
Decline towards death,

When we are compelled
To ask a question:

Is it an act of courage
Or cowardice,
To choose the time and place
Of one's own end?

An act of love
Or selfishness,
To ask our loved ones
To let us pass,
Rather than vainly
Resist our demise?

An act of compassion
Towards ourselves,
Or a violation
Of nature's way,
To choose a dignified death,
Free from pain?

"I do now let loose my opinion, hold it no longer."

Trinculo, *The Tempest*, 2.2.34

We all have lots of opinions—
Opinions that we've held so long
That we consider them to be facts;
Opinions that we hold so dear
That we think of them as truth;

But opinions aren't facts,
And opinions aren't truth—
Opinions are merely thoughts,
Mustered by the mind
To make sense of the world;

Opinions are just beliefs
Gathered by our egos
To help us to navigate our way
From day to day;

And if, just for a moment,
We could let loose our opinions,
Hold them no longer,
And notice what's around us—

A little girl spinning in a dress,
A cicada chirping in a tree,
A woolen scarf against our neck,
A splash of lemon in our tea,
A whiff of autumn in the air,

We might begin to understand
How our cherished opinions
Are not the least bit solid or real,
But are delusions that imprison us
In a perpetual state of judgment,
And prevent us from seeing the world
As it simply is.

> **"This above all: to thine own self be true."**
>
> Polonius, *Hamlet*, 1.3.78

When water is spilled,
It splatters and puddles—
But it is still water.

When water is heated,
It becomes steam—
But it is still water;

When water is frozen,
It becomes ice—
But it is still water.

In this way,
Water teaches us
How to adjust to the conditions
That arise in our lives
Without losing our integrity;

That, above all,
We must learn to respond
To the forces that act upon us
While, to ourselves,
Remaining true.

"Love moderately: long love doth so."

Friar Lawrence, *Romeo and Juliet*, 2.6.14

As a parent,
Loving a child as she grows up
Requires a delicate balance:

Be affectionate—but don't smother;

Be supportive—but don't obsess;

Be involved—but don't hover;

Be firm—but don't dominate;

Be protective—but don't stifle;

Be present—but don't cling;

Be vigilant—but don't spy;

Be trusting—but don't neglect;

Be forgiving—but don't spoil.

By always taking the middle path—
The path of moderation—
Your child will learn
To do the same;

As will, perhaps,
Your child's children.

> "There is special providence in the fall of a sparrow."
>
> Hamlet, *Hamlet*, 5.2.219

Although
The seagull is more resourceful,
The woodpecker, more industrious,
The peacock, more colorful,
The swan, more graceful,
The hummingbird, quicker,
The ostrich, larger,
The eagle, grander,
The owl, wiser,

The common house sparrow
Is not less special
Than any of these birds,

For the sparrow
Is connected
To all living things,
Just as all bird-kind,

And when it dies,
The flow of the universe—

Just as it does
With more superlative birds—

Ever so gently,
Adjusts accordingly.

The same, of course,
Can be said
Of any one of us.

> "Small have continual plodders ever won,
> Save base authority from others' books."
>
> Berowne, *Love's Labor's Lost*, 1.1.86

When listening to experts
Expounding upon
One subject or another,

It's important to remember
That there's a difference

Between acquiring knowledge
And acquiring judgment,

Between possessing information
And possessing understanding,

Between speaking with authority
And speaking with sagacity,

Between achieving success
And achieving mastery;

It's important to remember,
When we listen to the learned,

That it's experience, not books,
That gives us wisdom.

> "How mightily sometimes we make us comforts
> of our losses!"
>
> First Lord, *All's Well That Ends Well*, 4.3.65

Through habit,
We sometimes cling
To our despair.

Like a mirror,
We look to our misery
To tell us who we are;

Like a photograph,
We look to our heartache
To show us where we've been;

Like a child's blanket,
We look to our sadness
To pacify us with the familiar;

Like a compass,
We look to our losses
To point us towards tomorrow;

Like a hot fire,
We look to our anger
To protect us from the darkness.

How hard it is
To let go of our misery
When it feels so comfortable,
So cozy and familiar!

"A light heart lives long."

Katherine, *Love's Labor's Lost*, 5.2.18

Medical studies have shown
What many knew all along:

That our attitude,
Our state of mind,
Our habitual thoughts,
Can affect our health.

If we regularly
Spread pessimism,
Spew criticism,
Voice bitterness,
Smear blame,
Vent rage,
We can make ourselves sick;

Whereas,
If we maintain
A curious eye,
A receptive ear,
A mindful tongue,
An appreciative nose,
And a nurturing touch,

Making our way
Through each day
With a buoyant heart,

We can live lives
Blessed with good health,
Happiness, and longevity—

Just as many knew all along.

"The raven chides blackness."

Ulysses, *Troilus and Cressida*, 2.3.211

We spend a lot of time and energy
Disliking other people—
Avoiding them, criticizing them,
And judging them.

But if we truly open our eyes
And take a good look
At all the things we say,
And all the ways we behave,

We'd probably see
That we say and do
Exactly the same things
As the people in our lives
That we really dislike,
That we privately chide.

Which should teach us
That the key to accepting others
Is first to accept ourselves,

To be honest with ourselves
About our flaws and failings,

To be kind with ourselves
About our defects and deficiencies,

And to forgive ourselves
For our delusions,

So that we can be honest,
And kind, and forgiving,

With others.

"What may be done? for now I feel compassion."

Duke Theseus, *The Two Noble Kinsmen*, 3.6.271

There is so much
Human suffering,

So much misery
And so much need,

In our neighborhood,
In our country,
And around the globe,

That many of us
Feel paralyzed.

We feel compassion,
But the scale of the task at hand
Seems impossibly large,
The adversity, intractable,
The misery, insurmountable.

What may be done?

One answer
Is to start with just one person:
Ourselves—

To see our own suffering,
To soften our own hearts,
And begin to feel compassion
For ourselves;

Then to extend that compassion
In the direction
Of someone else in need.

> "What's in a name? That which we call a rose
> By any other word would smell as sweet."
>
> Juliet, *Romeo and Juliet*, 2.2.43

As toddlers,
We yearn to learn
The names of every thing,

For knowing the name
Allows us to ask for a thing,
To talk about a thing, and eventually,
To think about a thing.

As adults, however,
The words we've learned in childhood
To help us distinguish
One thing from another thing
Can blind us—

Making it impossible to see a thing
For what it truly is.

So that, now, in thinking about things,
We must strive to unlearn
The names of things,

Obliterate the verbal frames
We've given things,
And contemplate how every thing
Is interconnected with every other thing;

For one thing is clear:

Nothing eternal
Can be named,

And nothing with a name
Can be eternal.

> "There is some soul of goodness in things evil,
> Would men observingly distill it out."
>
> King Henry, *Henry V*, 4.1.4

How easy it is
To proclaim that people
Whose ways we do not understand,
Whose desires stand
In opposition to our own,
Are evil.

If we observe, however,
That these same people
Often point their fingers back,
Calling us the evil ones—
It should give us pause.

The simple fact
That we blame one another
As the source of our pain,
The cause of misery,
Should teach us something
About our shared humanity;

For if both sides would take the time
To look beyond good and evil,

Would take a moment
To see a bit of themselves
In the other, and a bit of the other
In themselves,

We might discover that we are the other,
And the other is us.

Then making peace with the other
Might be as simple as making peace
With ourselves.

> "Glory is like a circle in the water,
>   Which never ceaseth to enlarge itself,
>   Till by broad spreading it disperse to nought."
>
> Joan de Pucelle, *Henry VI, Part One*, 1.2.133

Those who strive mightily
To obtain wealth and power,

Who sacrifice contentment
To seek out fame,

Who desperately attempt
To make a splash in life,

Rarely envision
The inevitable hour

When the ripples of glory
Radiate so far outward

That they become
Invisible

And are entirely
Forgotten.

"In nature there's no blemish but the mind."

Antonio, *Twelfth Night*, 3.4.367

The mind of man
Is nature's only natural enemy,

For only the human mind
Imagines ways
To subvert the natural order
Of things in nature.

Floods and forest fires,
Though catastrophic,
Renew naturally,
Restoring life;

But the mind of man,
Greedy and cunning,
Irreversibly destroys—

Damming rivers,
Clear cutting forests,
Removing mountain tops,
Blighting skies, soiling seas,
Ravaging the natural world
Beyond all recognition;

By which we can see that
Only those who are mindful
Of man's place in nature

Can prevent
The mindless devastation
Of nature

At the hands
Of the human mind.

> "Men that make
> Envy and crooked malice nourishment
> Dare bite the best."
>
> Archbishop Cranmer, *Henry VIII*, 5.2.78

When it comes to food,
We often hear the adage:
"You are what you eat!"

When it comes to the media,
The same thing can be said:
You will become what you consume.

We should be wary, then,
About the articles we read,
The programs that we watch,
And the pundits that we hear,

For when we ingest
A steady diet
Of bitter resentment,
Of sour hatred, of salted envy,
And of peppered rage,

Those toxins, digested,
Become a part of us,
Enter our very cells,

And our bodies,
Trying to expel these poisons
Will vent them in every direction,

Even at those
Who deserve our malice least:

Those who love us best.

> **"We are such stuff**
>   **As dreams are made on; and our little life**
>   **Is rounded with a sleep."**
>
> Prospero, *The Tempest*, 4.1.156

We walk through life
As if in dream—

Not seeing
What's right in front of us,
But watching the shadows cast
By our most potent desires;

Not hearing
The sounds that surround us,
But listening to the clamor
Of our needs and hopes,
The incessant whispering
Of our phobias and fears.

We walk through life
Not actually present,
But replaying the past
And foretelling the future.

We walk through life
Dawdling in a fictional fog,
Unable to see the truth
Behind the misty delusions
Created by our minds.

And then, all too soon,
Often without ever waking,
The remainder of our little life
Is rounded off,
And we fall asleep
Forever.

> "If circumstances lead me, I will find
> Where truth is hid, though it were hid indeed
> Within the center."
>
> Polonius, *Hamlet*, 2.2.157

In making big decisions
We sometimes
Make ourselves crazy;

We tend to over-think things—
Let our minds lead us
Down blind alleys
And into dark mazes
Where we become lost.

But when we are sensitive
To our circumstances
And listen to our intuition,

The proper way
To the center of things
Will unfold in front of us,
Spontaneously, naturally, freely,

And difficult decisions
Suddenly make themselves.

"What, must I hold a candle to my shames?"

Jessica, *The Merchant of Venice*, 2.6.41

We tend to hide
The things about ourselves
That make us feel ashamed—

Concealing our insecurities,
Disguising our obsessions,
Shrouding our selfishness—

Not only from other people,
But from ourselves,

Making it challenging
To understand the reasons why
We say the things we say
And do the things we do;

Which means,
If we seek to say and do better,
We must illuminate our shames:

Hold a candle to our insecurities,
Turn a lamp on our obsessions,
Pour sunlight on our selfishness—

Not by way of confession,
Or to receive absolution,

But by way of observation,
As a means of navigation,

So we can begin to see
The way out of the darkness

Towards enlightenment.

> "The ground that gave them first has them again:
> Their pleasures here are past, so is their pain."
>
> Belarius, *Cymbeline*, 4.2.289

When a loved one dies
We mourn, quite naturally.

But if, even in our distress,
We can look back to the source
Of our loved one's being—
Not just before she was born
But before she was a thought—

We can see
That the same process
That made her birth possible—
That transformed her
From infinite nothingness
Into a miraculous, beloved
Something—

Now,
Using the very same process,
Transforms her back
To eternal nothingness,
Where neither
The pursuit of pleasure
Nor the avoidance of pain
Can trouble her.

Why then do we lament?

For this event that we call death
Is merely a moment in a process
As natural and as fluid

As the snow melting
To the ground in the spring.

> **"A turn or two I'll walk**
> **To still my beating mind."**
>
> Prospero, *The Tempest*, 4.1.162

How do we calm down
When we're feeling overwhelmed?
Walk.

How do we become aware
Of our negative, toxic thoughts?
Walk.

How do we become mindful
Of our untamed emotions?
Walk.

How do we bring ourselves
Back to the present moment?
Walk.

How do we reconnect
With our bodies and our breathing?
Walk.

How do we restore
Our innate sense of balance?
Walk.

How do we reawaken
To our place in the natural world?
Walk.

How do we set aside
Our daily trials and experience joy?
Walk.

Just walk.

"He that dies pays all debts."

Stephano, *The Tempest*, 3.2.131

There is no point
In seeking compensation
From the dead
For past injustices:

Railing upon
A dead father's temper or
A dead mother's drinking
Will profit you nothing;

Denouncing
A dead sister's selfishness or
A dead brother's recklessness
Won't change the past;

Dwelling upon
A dead friend's lies or
A dead partner's stealing
Won't undo their acts:

They have settled all their earthly accounts;

They can owe you nothing.

You owe it to yourself to drop it,
And spend the rest of your time
Indebted to them, grateful to them,
For teaching you
To refrain from causing others harm
As they did.

"A man's life's no more than to say 'one.'"

        Hamlet, *Hamlet*, 5.2.74

If scientists are correct,
Our universe was created
Fourteen billion years ago,
And has been expanding relentlessly
Ever since.

If this is so,
One person's time on this planet,
In this solar system,
This galaxy, this universe,

Is nothing but
An infinitesimally small
Non-event.

Yet, rather than debilitate us,
This understanding should liberate us—

Illuminate the proper scale of our daily trials
In the larger context of
Space/time.

When troubled, then, with misfortune,
And overwhelmed by worry,

Simply think of our universe,
Relentlessly expanding
For billions of years,
Inhale deeply, and say:

"One."

> **"Falsehood is worse in kings than beggars."**
>
> Imogen, *Cymbeline*, 3.6.13

Although all lies
Can be denounced as wrong,

All lies are not created equal—

For the greater the power
Of the individual,
The greater the impact
Of the lie.

So, by this reasoning,

The lie of a child
Is like an umbrella
That casts a shadow
Over the child alone,

The lie of an adult
Is like a cloud
That casts a shadow
Over everyone nearby,

And the lie of a king
Is like an eclipse
That blocks out the sun
Entirely.

"Good reasons must of force give place to better."

Brutus, *Julius Caesar*, 4.3.203

We live in a time
When our beliefs divide us.

We cling to our opinions,
And to our judgments,
The way a drowning man
Clings to a life preserver
In a churning sea.

But when a boat comes by
To offer a drowning man
A hand up
Out of the cold water,

Does it make any sense
For that same drowning man
To refuse to let go
Of the life preserver—

Even if it has saved him
From sinking?

"This music mads me, let it sound no more."

King Richard, *Richard II*, 5.5.61

Ever have a tune stuck in your head?
One that, once heard,
Persists in your mind's ears,
Playing itself over and over again
All day long?

Negative thoughts are like that, too:
They get stuck in our heads
And play themselves repeatedly—

Not just all day, but sometimes
For weeks, months, even years on end,
Until they drive us mad.

How do we prevent these thoughts—
Judgmental, bitter, angry thoughts—
From taking over our minds?

As with a catchy tune,
Commanding them to stop
Just doesn't work.

Instead, we must replace
These jarring strains
With other sounds—

With refrains of patience,
Songs of generosity,
Choruses of kindness,
Ballads of compassion—

Until the music
In our minds
Become instruments
Of love.

"The devil can cite scripture for his purpose."

Antonio, *The Merchant of Venice*, 1.3.98

As
A knowledge of the bible
Does not guarantee virtue,

And
A knowledge of the law
Does not guarantee justice,

And
A knowledge of ethics
Does not guarantee integrity,

And
A knowledge of the land
Does not guarantee stewardship,

And
A knowledge of human nature
Does not guarantee compassion,

And
A knowledge of books
Does not guarantee judgment,

So,
A knowledge of ourselves
Does not guarantee wisdom,

For
Such knowledge can be cited—
Chapter and verse—

To justify our purposes
Both good and ill.

"Nothing is but what is not."

Macbeth, *Macbeth*, 1.3.141

Look around you—what do you see?
What are the things, the tangible objects,
That surround you?

Now consider this:
Nothing that you see is permanent;
Nothing that you see is enduring;
Everything you see is in a state of flux—
Deteriorating, dissolving, changing,
On its way to becoming something else,
Something other than what it is.

Now look around again—
This time, not at the tangible objects,
But at the spaces in between,
At the nothingness that surrounds these things,
At the emptiness in which you are immersed;

Perceive what is not.

Wrap your mind around this nothingness;
Embrace the presence of this emptiness;
For this nothingness, this emptiness,
Is permanent, enduring, everlasting:
All things come from it,
And all things return to it.

Contemplate that everything you see—
All that is—
Is nothing more than an insubstantial bubble,
An illusion of time,
While everything you can't see—
All that is not—

Is all there truly is.

> "They say best men are molded out of faults,
> And, for the most, become much more the better
> For being a little bad."
>
> Marianna, Measure for Measure, 5.1.442

To be human is to be flawed—
There's no question about that.

The real question
Is not whether we have faults,
For we most certainly do,
But whether we have learned from them.

Have we learned
To acknowledge our faults
With grace?

Have we learned
To accept our faults
Without blaming someone else?

Have we learned
To consider those who point out our faults
As our strongest allies?

Have we learned
To look at our faults
As our greatest teachers?

Have we learned
To study our faults
As our most vital life lessons?

This is the way to know ourselves:

To become a little better
From being a little bad.

> "Who seeks, and will not take when once 'tis offered,
> Shall never find it more."
>
> Menas, *Antony and Cleopatra*, 2.7.83

We all seek joy in our lives,
We all seek happiness and contentment;

Sadly though, we often fail to see
The myriad of opportunities life offers
To experience these things
Every single day.

Minute by minute,
We're so engrossed in
Pursuing our goals,
Chasing our dreams,
Following our ambitions,

That we fail to see
What is right here
Within our grasp
At every moment.

Fail to accept
The beauty and the wonder
Being offered right now.

And it's possible,
In just this way,
To miss every opportunity
That life sends our way—

That is,
Except for the one big opportunity
Nobody can miss.

"The sense of death is most in apprehension."

Isabella, *Measure for Measure*, 3.1.77

Though we sometimes ponder
What we were
Before we were born,

Where we came from,
And how we came to be,

How our atoms and our cells
Gathered to become
The present form
That we call "me,"

There's never a sense of fear
That comes from our questioning—

Only a sense of wonderment.

As we ponder our death, then,
What we'll be after we die,

Where our atoms and our cells will go
When we have ceased to be,

There's no need to fear
The answers to our questions,

For the answers
Are precisely the same
As those about our birth,

And should be asked
With the same
Sense of wonderment.

> "Now bless thyself: thou met'st with things dying,
> I with things new-born."
>
> Shepherd, *The Winter's Tale*, 3.3.113

A new-born baby
Can be a blessing
At a funeral;

For a little baby,
Held lovingly
In the arms of its mother—

More than any words
Spoken by mourners,
Sung by choirs,
Or printed on memorials—

Lays bare the eternal truth:

That birth and death
Define one another.

"Love and be silent."

> Cordelia, *King Lear*, 1.1.62

A child learning to walk
Must be allowed to fall;

A teenager learning to drive
Must sit behind the wheel;

A young adult going off to college
Must leave the house;

A young man of marriageable age
Must choose his own spouse.

We are often tempted
To interfere with a child's endeavors—

It's hard to say nothing
And let them learn for themselves;

Yet that is what it is
To be a parent:

Love and be silent.

"That that is, is."

Feste, Twelfth Night, 4.2.13

Rather than simply accept what is,

We keep trying to resist what is,
To oppose what is, to change what is.

We do this
Even though we know perfectly well
That we have no choice,

That our lives unfold in the present,
In this very moment,

Not in the past or in the future,
But in this instant.

So we must learn
To be like children once again,

To focus on the present
And see the way things are right now,

To give ourselves over
To whatever this moment brings,

To flow with what is.

We don't have to like what is,
But we do have to accept what is,

Because what is, is—

And refusing to accept that that is
Does nothing whatsoever to change what is—

Except increase our suffering.

"You press me far, and therefore I will yield."

Portia, *The Merchant of Venice*, 4.1.425

In our hyper-competitive culture,
We tend to think of yielding
As surrender, as capitulation, as defeat.

To this way of thinking,
There are only winners and losers:
Yielding is a humiliation,
Yielding is an embarrassment,
Yielding is a failure.

These thoughts, however,
Are not borne out by nature.

Does a fish surrender to the river
When swimming downstream
To the sea?

Does the aspen tree capitulate to the wind
When its leaves shimmer
And its body sways?

Does the night defeat the sun
When it spreads across
One half of the earth?

In nature,
Yielding means cooperating,
Yielding means balancing,
Yielding means coexisting;

And are we not,
As human beings,
A part of nature?

> "O time, thou must untangle this, not I;
> It is too hard a knot for me to untie."
>
> Viola, *Twelfth Night*, 2.2.40

There are some problems
That cannot be unraveled
By immediate action—

They require time
Rather than doing,

Patience
Rather than performance,

Poise
Rather than effort.

So the next time
An impossible knot
Presents itself,

Instead of attacking it
With nails and teeth,

Try setting it aside,

Letting time take action,
While quietly applying

Non-action.

> "Nor I, nor any man that but man is,
>   With nothing shall be pleased, till he be eased
>   With being nothing."
>
>   Richard, *Richard II*, 5.5.39

Many of us search for happiness in our lives
By trying frantically
To make something of ourselves.

We strive to acquire title, or position,
Fame, wealth, power, authority, or respect,
Thinking that these things
Will bring us contentment;

But, as every one of these things
Is illusory, transitory, impermanent,
Subject to constant change,
Our efforts are preordained to fail.

Rather than trying frantically
To make something of ourselves,
We would do better to try quietly
To make nothing of ourselves;

For it is impossible to find
Contentment in this life
Until you are ready to accept

That nothing lasting
Can ever be accomplished,

That nothing you own
Can truly be possessed,

That we came from nothing,
And will return to nothing.

Finding ease in these eternal precepts
Is the portal to earthly joy.

"Youth's a stuff 'twill not endure."

Feste, *Twelfth Night*, 2.3.52

Though our youth,
Once it slips away,
Can never be regained,

Youthfulness can endure.

Though the eyes blur,
The hearing dulls,
The joints creak,
The muscles weaken,

We can remain curious,
And continue to learn;
We can stay engaged,
In the present—

With an infant's wonder,
A toddler's determination,
An adolescent's openness,
A teenager's fearlessness,
A twenty-something's gusto,
A thirty-something's assurance—

All the while smiling,
Laughing, and loving,
As if our supply of life
Were bottomless.

For the true
Stuff of youth

Is joy.

"Is it not strange that desire should so many years outlive performance?"

Poins, *Henry IV, Part Two*, 2.4.260

One might think
That aging would teach us
It is our ceaseless desire
That causes us to suffer—

Not just sexual desire,
But desire for praise,
Desire for fame,
Desire for pleasure,
Desire for gain.

Yet isn't it strange
That even when our health
Begins to fade,

Even when our aims
Cannot be enjoyed
If somehow obtained,

Many of us still cling
To our earthly desires
As if they would cure us
Of our ills?

As if they were
The air in our lungs
And the blood in our veins?

"O virtuous fight,
When right with right wars who shall be most right!"

Troilus, *Troilus and Cressida*, 3.2.171

All over the world,
People are convinced
That their beliefs are right—

So much so,
That they are willing
To fight for them,
To bleed for them,
To kill for them,
To die for them.

Throughout history,
Humans have pitted
Belief against belief,
Virtue against virtue,
Faith against faith,
Truth against truth,

Destroying untold lives
In the service of righteousness.

To break this cycle,
It is up to each one of us
To overcome our habit
Of taking sides,
Of seeing everything
As absolute opposites,

And seek the middle way
Where everything
Is both left and right,
Both up and down,
Both dark and light,
And where every side
Is our side.

"The good I stand on is my truth and honesty."

Archbishop Cranmer, *Henry VIII*, 5.1.122

To speak the truth
Regardless of status;

To honor promises
Despite inconvenience;

To give generously
Without thought of return;

To forgive injury
Without animosity;

To remain honest
While surrounded by fraud;

To show compassion,
Overcoming all reticence;

To love others,
Discounting all difference;

To do the right thing
Without even thinking:

This is integrity.

And though we are all
Born with it,

How many of us
Learn to stand on it?

Manage to die with it?

> "**Whether we shall meet again I know not;
> Therefore our everlasting farewell take.**"
>
> Brutus, *Julius Caesar*, 5.1.114

We live most of our lives
As if time were abundant,
Friends were everlasting,
Family, immortal.

But if, at each parting,
We were to think—

"This may be the last time
I'll lay my eyes upon you,

The last time
I'll hear your voice,

The last time
We'll embrace"—

Would we open our hearts
To all experience?

Accept all things
That come to us?

Live each moment
In the present?

> "In nature's infinite book of secrecy,
> A little I can read."
>
> Soothsayer, *Antony and Cleopatra*, 1.2.10

How do we learn
To grasp
What is ungraspable?

Perceive the form
Of what is formless?

Fathom the bounds
Of what is boundless?

Comprehend the fullness
Of what is empty?

Understand the presence
Of what is absent?

Sense the eternal
In a single moment?

First, we must learn—

With patience,
And with dedication—

How to read
What is unreadable:

Nature's infinite book of secrecy.

"Brevity is the soul of wit."

Polonius, *Hamlet*, 2.2.90

If wit
Is the ability
To express
Contradictory ideas
In short-lived bursts,

Perhaps human beings
Are nature's attempt
To be witty?

> "**Men must endure**
> **Their going hence even as their coming hither.**"
>
> Edgar, *King Lear*, 5.2.11

As we have no memory
Of our birth into this world—

No sense of the pain
Of being banished
From the warmth and safety
Of our own fluid universe,

No recollection
Of the sudden intense cold,
And the bright lights,
And the gloved hands,

No remembrance
Of the cutting of cord,
Or the poking of nurses,
Or the prodding of doctors,

No awareness
Of shaking with fear,
Or wailing for a bosom,
Or clamoring for sleep,

We have every reason to believe
That when we leave this world
And are born into the next,

No impression of that passage
Will remain with us,

Only profound gratitude
That loving souls were present

To help us on our way.

> "Like as the waves make towards the pebbled shore,
> So do our minutes hasten to their end."
>
> Sonnet 60, 1

When we see a photograph
Of our younger selves,
And note how much
We've changed,

We realize
That our perception
Of the passage of time
Is tremendously undependable,
Absurdly unreliable.

And because this is so,
We need to remember
To connect everyday
With things in nature
That show us the movement
Of the universe:

Clouds forming and reforming overhead;

Waves rolling in on the beach;

Leaves turning color in the fall;

Flowers sprouting in the spring.

These things remind us,
In the here and now,
Of the brevity of life,

And gently urge us
To spend our minutes

Wisely.

INDEX

INDEX OF SHAKESPEAREAN QUOTATIONS

All's Well That Ends Well 22, 130, 142

Antony and Cleopatra 28, 46, 125, 164, 177

As You Like It 24, 52, 53, 59, 73

The Comedy of Errors 6

Cymbeline 95, 127, 154, 158

Hamlet 31, 37, 54, 99, 119, 120, 136, 138, 140, 152, 157, 178

Julius Caesar 13, 23, 39, 44, 83, 107, 159, 176

King Henry IV, Part One 61, 78

King Henry IV, Part Two 12, 32, 50, 79, 106, 173

King Henry V 4, 69, 89, 101, 147

King Henry VI, Part One 92, 148

King Henry VI, Part Two 7, 18, 29, 33, 55, 67, 80

King Henry VI, Part Three 20, 131

King Henry VIII 8, 17, 35, 90, 150, 175

King John 91, 93

King Lear 36, 41, 56, 65, 85, 109, 112, 123, 129, 135, 167, 179

King Richard II 57, 81, 87, 108, 111, 160, 171

King Richard III 49

Love's Labor's Lost 10, 27, 48, 141, 143

Macbeth 5, 42, 100, 134, 162

Measure for Measure 11, 43, 62, 74, 113, 163, 165

The Merchant of Venice 14, 76, 86, 96, 103, 115, 117, 153, 161, 169

The Merry Wives of Windsor 84

A Midsummer Night's Dream 2, 30, 58, 77, 105, 121

Much Ado About Nothing 3, 38, 68, 70, 102, 128

Othello 19, 34, 40, 47, 60, 110, 132

Pericles 21, 71, 82, 94

The Rape of Lucrece 26

Romeo and Juliet 16, 25, 64, 122, 139, 146

Sonnets 63, 66, 116, 124, 126, 180

The Tempest 15, 133, 137, 151, 155, 156

Timon of Athens 88, 98, 104

Troilus and Cressida 1, 9, 45, 72, 144, 174

Twelfth Night 75, 97, 114, 118, 149, 168, 170, 172

The Two Noble Kinsmen 51, 145

The Winter's Tale 166

Made in the USA
Middletown, DE
10 April 2017